EVERYBODY COUNTS

A Report to the Nation on the Future of Mathematics Education

Mathematical Sciences Education Board

Board on Mathematical Sciences

Committee on the Mathematical Sciences in the Year 2000

National Research Council

NATIONAL ACADEMY PRESS
Washington, D.C.
1989

NATIONAL ACADEMY PRESS • 2101 Constitution Avenue, N.W. • Washington, D.C. 20418

NOTICE: The project that is the subject of this report was approved by the Governing Board of the National Research Council, whose members are drawn from the councils of the National Academy of Sciences, the National Academy of Engineering, and the Institute of Medicine. The members of the committees responsible for the report were chosen for their special competences and with regard for appropriate balance.

This report has been reviewed by a group other than the author according to procedures approved by a report review committee consisting of members of the National Academy of Sciences, the National Academy of Engineering, and the Institute of Medicine.

The National Research Council was organized by the National Academy of Sciences in 1916 to associate the broad community of science and technology with the Academy's purposes of furthering knowledge and advising the federal government. The Research Council functions in accordance with general policies determined by the Academy under the authority given to it in 1863 by its congressional charter, which established the Academy as a private, nonprofit, self-governing membership corporation. The Research Council is the principal operating agency of both the National Academy of Sciences and the National Academy of Engineering in providing services to the government, the public, and the scientific and engineering communities. It is administered jointly by both Academies and the Institute of Medicine. Dr. Frank Press and Dr. Robert M. White are chairman and vice chairman, respectively, of the National Research Council.

The Mathematical Sciences Education Board was established in 1985 to provide a continuing national overview and assessment capability for mathematics education and is concerned with excellence in mathematical sciences education for all students at all levels. The board reports directly to the Governing Board of the National Research Council.

The National Research Council created the Board on Mathematical Sciences in 1984. The objectives of the board are to maintain awareness and active concern for the health of the mathematical sciences and to serve as the focal point in the Research Council for issues connected with research in the mathematical sciences. Designed to conduct studies for federal agencies and to maintain liaison with the mathematical sciences communities, the board is part of the Commission on Physical Sciences, Mathematics, and Resources.

The Committee on the Mathematical Sciences in the Year 2000, which was appointed at the beginning of 1988, is a three-year joint project of the Mathematical Sciences Education Board and the Board on Mathematical Sciences. Its purpose is to provide a national agenda for revitalizing mathematical sciences education in U.S. colleges and universities.

Publication and dissemination of this book were supported by grants from Exxon Education Foundation, National Aeronautics and Space Administration, National Institutes of Health, National Research Council, National Science Foundation (Directorates for Biological and Behavioral and Social Sciences; Computer and Information Science and Engineering; Engineering; Geosciences; Mathematical and Physical Sciences; and Science and Engineering Education), Shell Oil Company Foundation, The Teagle Foundation, U.S. Department of Defense (Air Force Office of Scientific Research; Army Research Office; National Security Agency; Office of Naval Research), and U.S. Department of Energy. The observations made herein do not necessarily reflect the views of the grantors.

Library of Congress Cataloging-in-Publication Data

Everybody Counts: A Report to the Nation on the Future of Mathematics Education / Board on Mathematical Sciences [and] Mathematical Sciences Education Board, National Research Council.
    p.   cm.
    Bibliography: p.
    ISBN 0-309-03977-0
    1. Mathematics—Study and teaching—United States. I. National Research Council (U.S.). Board on Mathematical Sciences. II. National Research Council (U.S.). Mathematical Sciences Education Board.
QA13.E94 1989   88-37684
510'.7'1073-dc19   CIP

Summaries of this report may be obtained from the Mathematical Sciences Education Board, 818 Connecticut Avenue, N.W., Washington, D.C. 20006.

Printed in the United States of America

FOREWORD

In response to the urgent national need to revitalize mathematics and science education, the National Research Council (NRC) has undertaken an examination of U.S. mathematics education from kindergarten through graduate study. Major studies being conducted for the NRC by the Mathematical Sciences Education Board, the Board on Mathematical Sciences, and their joint Committee on the Mathematical Sciences in the Year 2000 have the goals of identifying weaknesses in the present system as well as strengths to build on for the future.

Everybody Counts is a public preface to the work of these three NRC units and other national organizations with which the NRC is cooperating in the revitalization of mathematics education. It outlines in stark terms the seriousness of the situation facing our country, emphasizing how crucial it is for science, technology, and the economy of the nation that *all* students receive high-quality education in mathematics. Yet, it goes well beyond this.

Numerous reports have appeared in recent years analyzing the problems of American education. *Everybody Counts* could easily be just one more report, pointing to problems and recommending that somebody, somewhere, should do something. Several features distinguish this report from others:

- It examines mathematics education as all one system, from kindergarten through graduate school.

- It treats all the major components of the system, from curricula, teaching, and assessment to human resources and national needs.

- It does not merely identify problems, but also charts a general course for the future, outlining a national strategy for pursuing that course.

- It is not the final report of a commission, but the beginning of a process through which teachers, state and local authorities, and the varied constituencies of mathematics education can draw together in a sustained revitalization effort.

This report reflects the thinking of 70 leading Americans, among them classroom teachers; college and university faculty and administrators; research mathematicians and statisticians; scientists and engineers; mathematics supervisors; school principals; school superintendents; chief state school officers; school board members; members of state and local governments; and leaders of parent groups, business, and industry.

It also signals to the nation that—acting through the National Research Council—the National Academy of Sciences, the National Academy of Engineering, and the Institute of Medicine are prepared to participate actively in the long-term work of rebuilding mathematics education in the United States. Few other tasks are more important to our children and to our nation.

Frank Press
President, National Academy of Sciences
Chairman, National Research Council

MATHEMATICAL SCIENCES EDUCATION BOARD

COMMITTEE ON THE MATHEMATICAL SCIENCES IN THE YEAR 2000

J. Fred Bucy (Chairman), Chief Executive Officer, Texas Instruments Incorporated (retired)

Lida K. Barrett, Dean, College of Arts and Sciences, Mississippi State University

Maria Antonietta Berriozabal, Councilwoman, City of San Antonio

Ernest L. Boyer, President, Carnegie Foundation for the Advancement of Teaching

William Browder, Professor of Mathematics, Princeton University

Rita R. Colwell, Director, Maryland Biotechnology Institute, University of Maryland

John M. Deutch, Provost, Massachusetts Institute of Technology

Ronald G. Douglas, Dean, College of Physical Sciences and Mathematics, State University of New York, Stony Brook

Patricia A. Dyer, Vice President for Academic Affairs, Palm Beach Junior College

Lloyd C. Elam, Professor of Psychiatry, Meharry Medical College

Ramesh A. Gangolli, Professor of Mathematics, University of Washington

William E. Kirwan, Vice Chancellor for Academic Affairs and Provost, University of Maryland

Nancy J. Kopell, Professor of Mathematics, Boston University

Donald W. Marquardt, Consultant Manager, E. I. du Pont de Nemours and Company

David S. Moore, Professor of Statistics, Purdue University

Jaime Oaxaca, Vice President, Northrop Corporation

Moshe F. Rubinstein, Professor of Engineering and Applied Science, University of California, Los Angeles

Ivar Stakgold, Chairman, Department of Mathematical Sciences, University of Delaware

S. Frederick Starr, President, Oberlin College

Lynn Arthur Steen, Professor of Mathematics, St. Olaf College

David R. Johnson, Chairman, Department of Mathematics, Nicolet High School, Glendale, Wisconsin; liaison with the Mathematical Sciences Education Board

Staff

James A. Voytuk, Project Director

Bernard L. Madison, Project Director (through August 1988)

Therese A. Hart, Research Assistant

PREFACE

As science and technology have come to influence all aspects of life, from health and environment to financial affairs and national defense, so mathematics has come to be of vital importance to the educational agenda of our nation. Mathematics is the foundation of science and technology. Increasingly, it plays a major role in determining the strength of the nation's work force. Yet, evidence all around us shows that American students are not fulfilling their potential in mathematics education.

Three of every four Americans stop studying mathematics before completing career or job prerequisites. Most students leave school without sufficient preparation in mathematics to cope with either on-the-job demands for problem-solving or college expectations for mathematical literacy. Industry, universities, and the armed forces are thus burdened by extensive and costly demands for remedial education. Our country cannot afford continuing generations of students limited by lack of mathematical power to second-class status in the society in which they live. It cannot afford to weaken its preeminent position in science and technology.

The three units which we chair at the National Research Council have committed themselves to remedying this situation. As a first step, we commissioned Lynn Arthur Steen, professor of mathematics at St. Olaf College, to write a synthesis of the thinking developed through three years of analysis by the Mathematical Sciences Education Board, two years of involvement by the Board on Mathematical Sciences (which deals with research), and the first year of work by the Committee on the Mathematical Sciences in the Year 2000, which is concerned with college and university mathematics.

Everybody Counts describes various forces that impinge on mathematics and on education—computers, research, demography, competitiveness—and explains how each is a major force for change, and yet interactions among these forces produce a system that is peculiarly resistant to change. The problems are complex. While the facts are indisputable, there is not complete unanimity on interpretations, priorities, or proposed solutions, even within the scientific community. Nevertheless, change must come. When one compares the potential return on investment in education with the consequences of inaction, it becomes clear that we as a nation have no choice: we must improve the ways our children learn mathematics.

Not merely a cry for reform, *Everybody Counts* points to specific transitions which our nation's schools and colleges must make in their mathematics programs over the next two decades if they are to meet the needs of students and the country as well as the accelerating momentum of a grass-roots reform effort already well under way. It argues for development of a national support structure to undergird that effort and describes major pieces of such a structure to be put in place over the next year. Its intent is to seek a broad consensus on a national strategy for getting the job done. Throughout, it reflects our prime concern that, whatever any of us do as individuals or through organizations to improve education, we see our role as supporting the efforts of the central person who can bring about meaningful and lasting change: the teacher.

We take this opportunity to express our gratitude to Lynn Steen for applying his considerable writing talents to the task of creating *Everybody Counts*. He has described in eloquent language the complex issues of mathematics education with which we shall be grappling for years to come.

Shirley A. Hill
Chairman, Mathematical Sciences
    Education Board
Curators' Professor of Mathematics
    and Education
University of Missouri, Kansas City

Phillip A. Griffiths
Chairman, Board on Mathematical
    Sciences
Provost and James B. Duke
    Professor of Mathematics
Duke University

J. Fred Bucy
Chairman, Committee on the Mathematical
    Sciences in the Year 2000
Chief Executive Officer
Texas Instruments Incorporated (retired)

CONTENTS

OPPORTUNITY ... *tapping the power of mathematics*　　*1*

 Context for Change 2
 Mathematics for Tomorrow 4
 A Pump, Not a Filter 6
 Numeracy 7
 Attitudes 9
 Goals 11
 Students at Risk 12

HUMAN RESOURCES ... *investing in intellectual capital*　*17*

 Demographic Trends 18
 Minorities 20
 Women 21
 Disabled Persons 23
 Graduate Students 24
 Supply and Demand 26
 Equity and Excellence 28

MATHEMATICS ... *searching for patterns*　　*31*

 Our Invisible Culture 32
 From Abstraction to Application 33
 Computers 36
 The Mathematical Community 37
 Undergraduate Mathematics 39

CURRICULUM ... *developing mathematical power*　　*43*

 Philosophy 43
 Standards 45
 Elementary Education 46
 Secondary Education 48
 Higher Education 51

TEACHING ...*learning through involvement*   *57*

    Understanding Mathematics   57
    Learning Mathematics   58
    Engaging Students   59
    Impact of Computers   61
    Education of Teachers   63
    Resources   66
    Assessment   67

CHANGE ...*mobilizing for curricular reform*   *73*

    Challenges   73
    Counterproductive Beliefs   75
    The American Way   77
    Modern Mathematics   78
    Lessons from the Past   79
    Transitions   81

ACTION ...*moving into the 21st century*   *87*

    National Goals   88
    Reaching Consensus   89
    National Strategy   90
    Support Structures   91
    Leadership   93
    Taking Action   95

REFERENCES ...*documenting the challenge*   *99*

    Notes   99
    Sources   102
    Bibliography   104

EVERYBODY COUNTS

**A Report to the Nation
on the
Future of Mathematics Education**

OPPORTUNITY  *...tapping the power of mathematics*

Mathematics is the key to opportunity. No longer just the language of science, mathematics now contributes in direct and fundamental ways to business, finance, health, and defense. For students, it opens doors to careers. For citizens, it enables informed decisions. For nations, it provides knowledge to compete in a technological economy. To participate fully in the world of the future, America must tap the power of mathematics.

Communication has created a world economy in which working smarter is more important than merely working harder. Jobs that contribute to this world economy require workers who are mentally fit—workers who are prepared to absorb new ideas, to adapt to change, to cope with ambiguity, to perceive patterns, and to solve unconventional problems. It is *these* needs, not just the need for calculation (which is now done mostly by machines), that make mathematics a prerequisite to so many jobs. More than ever before, Americans need to think for a living; more than ever before, they need to think mathematically.

Quality mathematics education for all students is essential for a healthy economy.

Yet, for lack of mathematical power, many of today's students are not prepared for tomorrow's jobs. In fact, many are not even prepared for today's jobs. Current mathematical achievement of U.S. students is nowhere near what is required to sustain our nation's leadership in a global technological society. As technology has "mathematicized" the workplace and as mathematics has permeated society, a complacent America has tolerated underachievement as the norm for mathematics education. We have inherited a mathematics curriculum conforming to the past, blind to the future, and bound by a tradition of minimum expectations.

Wake up, America! Your children are at risk. Three of every four Americans stop studying mathematics before

"How can students compete in a mathematical society when they leave school knowing so little mathematics?"

—*Lester Thurow**

People, reports, and data cited in the margins are identified on pages 102–103.

Opportunity

completing career or job prerequisites. Most students leave school without sufficient preparation in mathematics to cope either with on-the-job demands for problem-solving or with college requirements for mathematical literacy. Thus, industry, universities, and the armed forces are burdened by extensive and costly demands for remedial education.

Today's mathematics opens doors to tomorrow's jobs. As successive waves of immigrants have used this country's educational system to secure better lives for themselves and their children, so today's children the world over are using mathematical training as a platform on which to build up their lives. America's children deserve the same chance.

Children *can* succeed in mathematics. Many do so in other countries and some do so in this country. The evidence from other nations shows overwhelmingly that if more is expected in mathematics education, more will be achieved. Clear expectations of success by parents, by schools, and by society can promote success by students.

C..
hildren *can* succeed in mathematics. If more is expected, more will be achieved.

....

In today's world, the security and wealth of nations depend on their human resources. So does the prosperity of individuals and businesses. As competitors get smarter, our problems get harder. Long-term investment in science and technology—both for businesses and for our nation—requires serious commitment to revitalizing mathematics education. It is time to act, to ensure that *all* Americans benefit from the power of mathematics.

Context for Change

In 1983, *A Nation at Risk* awoke a sleeping nation to alarming problems in our educational system. Since then, dozens of reports have analyzed virtually every aspect of this enormous problem. Some call for changes in curriculum, others for changes in the structure of schools; some cite deficiencies in the ways teachers are educated, while others examine signs of decay in the social and economic structures of society. All agree that the present system must change.

Mathematics education takes place in the context of schools. Like other subjects, mathematics is constrained by limits of school and society, of texts and tests. Much that needs improvement must be accomplished by systemic remedies that affect all subjects and all schools. Much is being done by school districts and community organizations, by legislatures and universities, by corporations and teachers. Nevertheless, much remains to be done.

Although mathematics is not unique in its importance to education, mathematics education tends to magnify many problems of the schools. Literature, history, science, and other subjects contribute in essential ways to a well-balanced education; no one can say that one field is intrinsically of greater worth than another. It is clear, however, that mathematics plays a special role in school education, one that is especially sensitive to deficiencies in the effectiveness of the educational system.

Since mathematics is the foundation of science and technology, it serves as a key to opportunity and careers. Moreover, mathematics contributes to literacy certain distinctive habits of mind that are of increasing importance to an informed citizenry in a technological age. Because of the fundamental importance of literacy and numeracy, English and mathematics are the only subjects taught continuously throughout the school years.

Education in any discipline helps students learn to think, but education also must help students take responsibility for their thoughts. While this objective applies to all subjects, it is particularly apt in mathematics education because mathematics is an area in which even young children can solve a problem and have confidence that the solution is correct—not because the teacher says it is, but because its inner logic is so clear.

"Reading, 'Riting, and ..."

Mathematics, of course, is not the *only* cornerstone of opportunity in today's world. Reading is even more fundamental as a basis for learning and for life. What is different today is the great increase in the importance of mathematics to so many areas of education, citizenship, and careers.

M

athematics is a key to opportunity and careers.

Educators no longer argue that mathematics trains the mind for clear thinking in other subjects. Mathematics does, however, provide one of the few disciplines in which the growing student can, by exercising only the power inherent in his or her own mind, reach conclusions with full assurance. More than most other school subjects, mathematics offers special opportunities for children to learn the power of thought as distinct from the power of authority. This is a very important lesson to learn, an essential step in the emergence of independent thinking.

Mathematics for Tomorrow

The increasing importance of mathematics to society is only one of many factors that compel special examination of mathematics education. Mathematics itself is now significantly more diverse than it was several decades ago when today's leaders and educators went to school. The arithmetic, algebra, geometry, and calculus taught nowadays are mere shadow images of modern mathematics. The mathematical sciences of today blend deep new results from these traditional areas with methods from such applied fields as statistics, operations research, and computer science. Modern mathematics provides a powerful instrument for understanding the world in which we live.

Several factors—growth of technology, increased applications, impact of computers, and expansion of mathematics itself—have combined in the past quarter century to extend greatly both the scope and the application of the mathematical sciences. Together, these forces have created a revolution in the nature and role of mathematics—a revolution that must be reflected in the schools if our students are to be well prepared for tomorrow's world. Education reflecting only

Myth: "There is no algebra in my future."

Reality: Just because students do not use algebra anywhere except in algebra class does not mean that they will not need mathematics in the future. Over 75 percent of all jobs require proficiency in simple algebra and geometry, either as a prerequisite to a training program or as part of a licensure examination.

the mathematics of the distant past is no longer adequate for present needs.

From the accountant who explores the consequences of changes in tax law to the engineer who designs a new aircraft, the practitioner of mathematics in the computer age is more likely to solve equations by computer-generated graphs and calculations than by manual algebraic manipulations. Mathematics today involves far more than calculation; clarification of the problem, deduction of consequences, formulation of alternatives, and development of appropriate tools are as much a part of the modern mathematician's craft as are solving equations or providing answers.

Statistics, the science of data, has blossomed from roots in agriculture and genetics into a rich mathematical science that provides essential tools both for analyses of uncertainty and for forecasts of future events. From clinical research to market surveys, from enhancement of digital photographs to stock market models, statistical methods permeate policy analysis in every area of human affairs.

Challenging problems in such diverse fields as computer science and social science have invigorated the discipline of discrete mathematics, a field that reflects both computer logic and human ambivalence. Moreover, new mathematical tools such as game theory and decision theory are being applied to the human sciences where one seeks to make choices, decisions, and coalitions on some rational and systematic basis.

A................................
pplications, computers, and new discoveries have extended greatly the landscape of mathematics.
....

Today's mathematics is a creative counterpoint of computation and deduction, rooted in data while unfolding in abstraction. Mathematics today is being continually created and adapted to meet new needs. Frequent interactions

Opportunity

Mathematics Pipeline

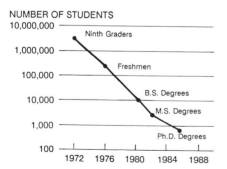

Data from enrollments in mathematics courses reveal that roughly half the students leave the pipeline each year.

among different specialties reveal deep connections and hidden unity, strongly suggesting that the different mathematical sciences are merely facets of a single science of patterns.

A Pump, Not a Filter

The revolution in the way that mathematics is practiced is mirrored by a similar—but unfulfilled—revolution in our understanding of how students actually learn mathematics. Research on learning shows that most students cannot learn mathematics effectively by only listening and imitating; yet most teachers teach mathematics just this way. Most teachers teach as they were taught, not as they were taught to teach.

Research in learning shows that students actually construct their own understanding based on new experiences that enlarge the intellectual framework in which ideas can be created. Consequently, each individual's knowledge of mathematics is uniquely personal. Mathematics becomes useful to a student only when it has been developed through a personal intellectual engagement that creates new understanding. Much of the failure in school mathematics is due to a tradition of teaching that is inappropriate to the way most students learn.

We require students to study mathematics for many reasons: to learn practical skills for daily lives, to understand quantitative aspects of public policy, to develop problem-solving skills, and to prepare for careers. None of these goals is being achieved; not only do we face a shortage of personnel with mathematical preparation suitable to scientific and technological jobs, but also the level of mathematical literacy (or "numeracy") of the general public is completely inadequate to reach either our personal or national aspirations.

Mathematics education is an immense enterprise, involving over 10 percent of the nation's educational resources—about $25 billion annually. Each year, 25 million elementary school children, 10 million secondary school students, and 3 million undergraduates study mathematics; indeed, about 60 percent of school-level and 30 percent of college-level science and technology education are devoted to mathematics.

Mathematics must become a pump rather than a filter in the pipeline of American education.

Everyone depends on the success of mathematics education; everyone is hurt when it fails.

More than any other subject, mathematics filters students out of programs leading to scientific and professional careers. From high school through graduate school, the half-life of students in the mathematics pipeline is about one year; on average, we lose half the students from mathematics each year, although various requirements hold some students in class temporarily for an extra term or a year. Mathematics is the worst curricular villain in driving students to failure in school. When mathematics acts as a filter, it not only filters students out of careers, but frequently out of school itself.

Low expectations and limited opportunity to learn have helped drive dropout rates among Blacks and Hispanics *much* higher—unacceptably high for a society committed to equality of opportunity. It is vitally important for society that *all* citizens benefit equally from high-quality mathematics education.

Numeracy

To function in today's society, mathematical literacy—what the British call "numeracy"—is as essential as verbal literacy. These two kinds of literacy, although different, are not unrelated. Without the ability to read and understand, no one can become mathematically literate. Increasingly, the reverse is also true: without the ability to understand basic mathematical ideas, one cannot fully comprehend modern writing such as that which appears in the daily newspapers.

Numeracy requires more than just familiarity with numbers. To cope confidently with the demands of today's society, one must be able to grasp the implications of many

"Numeracy is the ability to cope confidently with the mathematical demands of adult life."
—*Mathematics Counts*

7

mathematical concepts—for example, chance, logic, and graphs—that permeate daily news and routine decisions.

Literacy is a moving target, increasing in level with the rising technological demands of society. Indeed, there is some evidence that the decline in reading comprehension scores over the last several decades is due in part to the growing mathematical content of what one is required to read. It is not just computer manuals or financial reports that require an understanding of mathematical ideas; so do reports of political polls, debates about AIDS testing, and arguments over the federal deficit. Even Supreme Court decisions resemble mathematical arguments whose subject matter is law rather than numbers; often, legal cases rest as much on probabilistic inferences (for example, DNA fingerprinting, fiber analysis) as on direct evidence.

Mathematical literacy is essential as a foundation for democracy in a technological age.

Functional literacy in all of its manifestations—verbal, mathematical, scientific, and cultural—provides a common fabric of communication indispensable for modern civilized society. Mathematical literacy is especially crucial because mathematics is the language of science and technology. Discussion of important health and environmental issues (acid rain, waste management, greenhouse effect) is impossible without using the language of mathematics; solutions to these problems will require a public consensus built on the social fabric of literacy.

The study of mathematics can help develop critical habits of mind—to distinguish evidence from anecdote, to recognize nonsense, to understand chance, and to value proof. Citizens in a democracy must recognize that change is a process with expected regularities; that order can beget disorder (as in turbulence) and vice versa (as in statistical experiments); that similar mathematical models can represent different phenomena (for example, patterns of growth in biology, economics, and chemistry); and that simple models can clarify complex systems (as in linear models of economic systems), even though simplistic analysis can result in misleading interpretations. Citizens who are bombarded daily with conflicting quantitative information need to be aware of both the power and the limitations of mathematics.

The great majority of American children spend most of their school mathematics time learning only practical arithmetic. Few retain much of what they learn about geometry; fewer still learn anything about chance. Secondary education is particularly devoid of exposure to modes of mathematical thought required for intelligent citizenship. Even colleges and universities seem unable to infuse appropriate mathematical ideas into liberal education. There is no consensus whatsoever on a collegiate mathematics curriculum for students outside the preprofessional programs where mathematics serves a well-defined yet strictly utilitarian purpose. Rarely does mathematics contribute as it should to liberal education, to the honing of values, and to effective citizenship.

Attitudes

One of the more disturbing conclusions of recent studies of mathematics education is that the American public tends to assume that differences in accomplishment in school mathematics are due primarily to differences in innate ability rather than to differences in individual effort or in opportunity to learn. These beliefs surface in many ways—in studies of parents' views, in common self-deprecating remarks ("I never could do math"), and in public infatuation with early tracking as a strategy for mathematics education.

One consequence of such beliefs is that parents often accept—and sometimes even expect—their children's poor performance in mathematics. Another consequence is that adults who determine policy in mathematics education often measure the mathematical needs of today's students by their

> *"We've inherited a woefully limited set of expectations of what schools can accomplish and what children can learn."*
> —*William R. Graham*

Myth: Learning mathematics requires special ability, which most students do not have.

Reality: Only in the United States do people believe that learning mathematics depends on special ability. In other countries, students, parents, and teachers all expect that most students can master mathematics if only they work hard enough. The record of accomplishment in these countries—and in some intervention programs in the United States—shows that most students can learn much more mathematics than is commonly assumed in this country.

own meager and outdated mathematical accomplishments. From the faulty premise that most students "can't do math" and the fact that many adults who never learned mathematics have succeeded without it, they rationalize that official expectations should be limited to minimal basic levels. The result is a spiral of lowered expectations in which poor performance in mathematics has become socially acceptable.

P . . . .
ublic acceptance of deficient standards contributes significantly to poor performance in mathematics education.
. . . .

Even worse, the unrestricted power of peer pressure often makes good performance in mathematics socially unacceptable. This environment of negative expectation is strongest among minorities and women—those most at risk—during high school years when students first exercise choice in curricular goals. Even strong positive support of adults is often powerless to open the eyes of children who are blinded by their entertainment-dominated culture.

Public attitudes about mathematics are shaped primarily by adults' childhood school experiences. Consequently, mathematics is seen not as something that people actually use, but as a best forgotten (and often painful) requirement of school. For most members of the public, their lasting memories of school mathematics are unpleasant—since so often the last mathematics course they took convinced them to take no more.

Some adults blame the "new math" for their fears, having become convinced of their own mathematical ineptitude by instruction steeped in premature abstraction. Others have been made apprehensive by a teacher's rigid view of mathematics as a string of procedures to be memorized, where right answers count more than right thinking. Either extreme—mindless abstraction or mindless calculation—yields mindless mathematics. These widespread fears reinforce common public perceptions that mathematicians are responsible for making mathematics hard and that only geniuses are capable of learning mathematics.

Children respond to expectations of their parents and teachers. It is no wonder that many students stop studying mathematics as soon as it becomes optional, since society provides so few hero-images for whom perseverance in mathematics has paid off. When parents think that ability supersedes effort, most students never learn the value of effort. "Hard work pays off" should be society's message to those who study mathematics.

Goals

Historically, schools in the United States were designed with a dual mission: to teach all students basic skills required for a lifetime of work in an industrial and agricultural economy and to educate thoroughly a small elite who would go to college en route to professional careers. As the needs of society have changed—as the fraction of students preparing to work in factories or on farms has declined—the balance of these two goals has shifted. Today's schools labor under the legacy of a structure designed for the industrial age misapplied to educate children for the information age.

Not only in mathematics but in every school subject, educators are faced with rising expectations for preparing the kind of work force the country will need in the future. Information-age technology will continue to grow in importance; pressed by rising international competition, industry will demand increased quality and increased productivity. The world of work in the twenty-first century will be less manual but more mental; less mechanical but more electronic; less routine but more verbal; and less static but more varied.

The changing nature of work will make continuing education a lifelong reality for adults. Schools, therefore, will have to provide all students with a strong foundation for lifelong learning; colleges and universities will have to educate both young adults and older workers; and industry will have to focus its continuing education on areas that extend rather

Back to School

A newspaper interested in a tax proposal conducted a poll using a random sample of 100 voters on each of two successive Mondays. The first week they found 57 percent in favor; in the second week, they found 59 percent in favor. The headline for its story read: "Support Grows for Tax Hike." Write a letter to the editor about this story.

Opportunity

I..
n the future, schools and colleges will need to meet goals that they now believe to be impossible.

....

than repeat what schools provide. Education in the future must build continually from childhood to retirement on a versatile foundation provided by school education.

Literacy and numeracy are the primary sources of strength and versatility in school education. As colleges, universities, and continuing education attract significant fractions of the population, schools must now prepare *all* students for some type of postsecondary study. The level of literacy formerly associated with the few who entered college must now be a goal for all.

Quantitative literacy provides the foundation of technological expertise in the workplace. The facility with mathematics formerly required only of those preparing for scientific careers is now an essential ingredient in the foundation for lifelong work in the information age. In tomorrow's world, the best opportunities for jobs and advancement will go to those prepared to cope confidently with quantitative, scientific, and technological issues. Mathematical power provides the key to these opportunities.

Students at Risk

Daunting as the challenge of reform appears, its cost is insignificant when compared with the consequences of inaction. Over 25 percent of all high school students drop out before graduating; although half of these students do eventually receive an equivalency diploma, their detour is costly for them and for society. Among Blacks, Hispanics, and Native Americans, the dropout rate often exceeds 50 percent.

The majority of those who drop out are functionally illiterate and hardly any of them possess enough mathematical skills to make productive contributions to the American economy. Dropouts and illiteracy are destroying individual

"We can improve. We can keep kids in school longer and achieve a better result. We cannot fail in education. If we fail, we fail our kids and we fail our future."

—*Jaime Escalante*

hope and threatening the foundation of this country's economy. Disparities that divide one third of our nation from the rest compromise quality of life for all citizens.

Industry spends as much on remedial mathematics education for employees as is spent on mathematics education in schools, colleges, and universities. In addition, 60 percent of college mathematics enrollments are in courses ordinarily taught in high school. This massive repetition is grossly inefficient, wasting resources that could be used better to improve rather than to repeat mathematics education.

We are at risk of becoming a nation divided both economically and racially by knowledge of mathematics.

"America is moving backward—not forward—in its efforts to achieve the full participation of minority citizens in the life and prosperity of the nation."
—*One Third of a Nation*

Broad-brush attempts to deal with underachievement in mathematics often aggravate the very problems they are trying to solve. Raising standards for graduation often widens the gap between those who know mathematics and those who do not, since increased standards are rarely accompanied by program changes to provide appropriate courses for students who are not motivated to study mathematics. Requirements designed to ensure that all students reach certain minimum levels often yield results in which most students reach *only* the minimum level—because rarely are schools given the resources necessary both to achieve minimum standards for all and to provide unlimited accomplishment for most.

Despite massive effort, relatively little is accomplished by remediation programs. No one—not educators, mathematicians, or researchers—knows how to reverse a consistent early pattern of low achievement and failure. Repetition rarely works; more often than not, it simply reinforces previous failure. The best time to learn mathematics is when it is first taught; the best way to teach mathematics is to teach it well the first time.

Opportunity

Apart from economics, the social and political consequences of mathematical illiteracy provide alarming signals for the survival of democracy in America. Because mathematics holds the key to leadership in our information-based society, the widening gap between those who are mathematically literate and those who are not coincides, to a frightening degree, with racial and economic categories. We are at risk of becoming a divided nation in which knowledge of mathematics supports a productive, technologically powerful elite while a dependent, semiliterate majority, disproportionately Hispanic and Black, find economic and political power beyond reach. Unless corrected, innumeracy and illiteracy will drive America apart.

HUMAN RESOURCES

...investing in intellectual capital

Evidence from many sources points to an impending shortage of mathematically trained personnel at every academic level, from high school graduates to Ph.D.'s. Too few students enter college prepared to undertake the study of mathematics necessary for their degree programs; too few graduate with mathematics degrees to meet the needs of secondary school teaching or industrial employment; and too few enter or complete graduate study to sustain the mathematical strength of universities and the research needs of our nation. Moreover, many segments of the American population are significantly underrepresented at every stage in the mathematics pipeline.

T o meet tomorrow's needs, we must invest today in our nation's intellectual capital.

The underrepresentation of minorities and women in scientific careers is well documented and widely known. Less widely known is the general underrepresentation of American students in all mathematically based graduate programs. Evidence of disinterest in mathematics permeates all racial, socioeconomic, and educational categories, although the level of disinterest varies greatly among different groups. Young Americans' avoidance of mathematics courses and careers arises from immersion in a culture that provides more alternatives than stimulants to the study of mathematics. Without motivation and effective opportunity to learn, few students of any background are likely to persevere in the study of mathematics.

As we enter a decade of decline in the number of college graduates, concerns of equity join common cause with those of economic need. Mathematical illiteracy both impedes socioeconomic equality and diminishes national productivity. It is a significant handicap from which neither the individual nor our nation can easily recover. The very magnitude of the problem has forged a new coalition for change based

Intended Mathematics Majors of Top High School Seniors

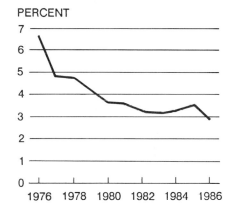

Since 1975, the percentage of top high school seniors who expressed an interest in majoring in mathematics or statistics has declined by over 50 percent, even as the corresponding percentage for science and engineering remained relatively constant.

17

Shifting Student Interests

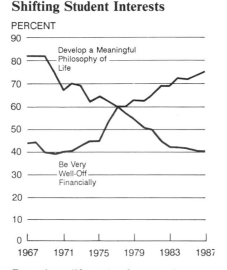

Data about life goals of college freshmen for the past quarter century show a consistent trend away from philosophical and scientific pursuits toward those that offer a promise of financial security.

"*White males, thought of only a generation ago as the mainstays of the economy, will comprise only 15 percent of the net additions to the labor force between 1985 and 2000.*"

—*Workforce 2000*

on shared interest between those who currently enjoy the benefits of mathematical power and those who do not.

Mathematical illiteracy is both a personal loss and a national debt.

Developing more mathematical talent for the nation will require fundamental change in education. Our national problem is not only how to nurture talent once it surfaces, but also how to make more talent rise to the surface. Although more must be done, the United States is reasonably successful in tapping and channeling the highly visible talent springs which develop without special support from formal schooling. But these sources are inadequate to our national need. We must, in addition, raise the entire water table. This is a much more massive problem, one that cannot be attacked successfully through thousands of disconnected little programs, beneficial as they may be for the individuals affected. Although small local programs do sometimes suggest directions for systemic change, too often their effects remain strictly local. To raise the water table of mathematical talent, we must understand and change the system as a whole.

Demographic Trends

During the next two decades, the number of 20- to 30-year-olds in the United States will decline by about 25 percent, even as the number of school-age children increases by a similar amount. Hence, the demand for mathematics teachers will rise just as the pool from which new teachers can be drawn will be shrinking.

In the long run, the most important factor affecting education is the changing profile of students. By the year 2000, one in every three American students will be minority; by 2020, today's minorities will become the majority of students in the United States. Of those under 18, the proportion of minorities is already nearing 40 percent, almost three times what it was just after World War II. Already, the ten largest school districts in the United States are 70 percent Black and Hispanic. Because of high birth rates and regular immigration, the Hispanic population in the United States is growing at five times the national average. For as far ahead as we can reliably project, the percentage of minority children in America will continue to grow.

In addition, according to Census Bureau estimates, 60 percent of children born in the 1980's will, before reaching the age of 18, live in a home with only one parent. More than one child in four comes from a family that lives in poverty; nearly one in five comes from a home in which English is not spoken; and one in three comes home to an empty house, with no adult to greet the child and encourage attention to homework. The children of today's high school dropouts are the high school students of the first decade of the twenty-first century.

The work force, too, is changing character. Whereas formerly 90 percent of the work force was White, between now and the beginning of the twenty-first century one in three new workers will be minority. Because of the general aging of the population as the postwar baby boom reaches retirement age, the United States will soon reach an all-time low in the number of workers per retiree; instead of 15 workers supporting every retiree, as there were in 1950, there will be only three.

Currently, 8 percent of the labor force consists of scientists or engineers; the overwhelming majority are White males. But by the end of the century, only 15 percent of net new entrants to the labor force will be White males. Changing demographics have raised the stakes for all Americans. Never before have we been forced to provide true equality in opportunity to learn. The challenge we face today is to achieve what we believe.

"Every day in America, 40 teen-age girls give birth to their third child."

—*Harold L. Hodgkinson*

19

Jaime Escalante, a teacher at Garfield High School in Los Angeles, shows what students can do when properly motivated. "I believe potential is everywhere." During the last ten years, hundreds of Escalante's students have passed the Advanced Placement calculus examination.

Voice of Experience

"Black engineering students were invited to join the Black Honors Calculus Society, where they were challenged with difficult problems. Where before they worked individually—not always successfully—now they meet and tackle much harder problems, working in teams of two or three."
—Uri Treisman

Minorities

Non-Asian minorities (Blacks, Hispanics, and Native Americans) are significantly underrepresented in all scientific, engineering, and professional fields. The extent of underrepresentation is in direct proportion to the amount of mathematics employed in the field. For lack of proper foundation in mathematics, Blacks, Hispanics, and Native Americans are shut out of many scientific and business careers.

Despite the growing size of the Black and Hispanic populations, comparatively few individuals in these communities take degrees in fields that require advanced mathematics. Of Americans who receive bachelor's, master's, and doctoral degrees in the physical sciences (including mathematics, physics, and engineering), 95 percent are Whites and Asians. During the last fifteen years, the total annual number of American Blacks and Hispanics receiving a doctoral degree in the mathematical sciences has averaged less than ten.

Although demographic factors influence all aspects of education, they affect mathematics education in especially troublesome ways. Among the many subjects taught in school, mathematics is probably the most universal, depending least on a student's background and culture. As a result, mathematics education has, with few exceptions, been generally exempt from public controversy based on religious or social views. Indeed, mathematics has benefited from widespread support of its value in general education. Yet at the same time, precisely because mathematics has few links to issues of belief, mathematical ideas are not transmitted in our culture in the same way as are theories of evolution or standards of ethics.

School mathematics should, therefore, transcend the cultural diversity of our nation. In fact, it does just the opposite. In the United States, mathematics is primarily part of upper- and middle-class male culture. Except for shopkeeper arithmetic of a bygone age taught in elementary school, few parts of mathematics are embedded in the family or cultural traditions of members of the many large "developing countries" that make up the American mosaic.

Indicators of achievement and aptitude support this general assessment. Students enrolled in advanced high school mathematics courses come disproportionately from White upper- and middle-class families. Differences in culture and parental expectation magnified by differential opportunities to learn imposed by twelve years of multiply tracked classes produce vastly different evidence of mathematical power.

Inadequate preparation in mathematics imposes a special economic handicap on minorities.

The long-term effect of minority underrepresentation in mathematics is magnified because so many mathematics professionals are teachers. During the next decade, 30 percent of public school children, but only 5 percent of their mathematics teachers, will be minorities. The inescapable fact is that two demographic forces—increasing Black and Hispanic youth in the classrooms, decreasing Black and Hispanic graduates in mathematics—will virtually eliminate classroom role models for those students who most need motivation, incentive, and high-quality teaching of mathematics. The underrepresentation of this generation of minorities leads to further underrepresentation in the next, yielding an unending cycle of mathematical poverty.

Women

For reasons that are deeply rooted in culture and tradition, men significantly outnumber women in mathematics-based careers. As students progress through the mathematics curriculum, girls and boys show little difference in ability, effort, or interest in mathematics until adolescent years when course and career choices begin influencing school effort. Then, as social pressure increases and career goals

"The issue of the full participation of women in science is at the very heart of the question of who will do science in the years ahead."

—*Sheila Widnall*

21

are formed, girls' decisions to reduce effort in the study of mathematics progressively cut women off from many professional careers.

Many women drop mathematics in high school or in the transition to college. Others drop out later. Women perform virtually as well as men in college mathematics courses, but beyond the bachelor's degree women drop out of mathematics at twice the rate of men and at twice the rate of women in other scientific disciplines. Women now enter college nearly as well prepared in mathematics as men, and 46 percent of mathematics baccalaureates go to women. Despite this record, only 35 percent of the master's degrees and 17 percent of the Ph.D. degrees in the mathematical sciences are earned by women.

Overall, women receive approximately one third of university degrees in science and engineering. The highest percentages of women are found in those sciences with the least mathematical prerequisites: psychology, biology, and sociology. The lowest percentages of women enter fields requiring the most mathematics, namely, physics, engineering, economics, geoscience, and chemistry. Evidence from many sources suggests that it is differences in course patterns rather than lack of ability that matter most in limiting women's access to careers in mathematically intensive sciences.

Widely reported studies concerning the high percentage of boys among mathematical prodigies—those who at age 12 perform at the level of average college students—often convey the impression that gender differences in mathematics are biologically determined. But evidence from the vast majority of students shows almost no difference in performance among male and female students who have taken equal advantage of similar opportunities to study mathematics. Inferences from very exceptional students—child prodigies—mean little about the performance of the general population.

Cross-national studies of gender differences in mathematics suggest that most of the differences observed are due to the accumulating effects of sex-role experiences at home, in school, and in society. The gender gap in mathematics widens with increasing exposure to school and society; moreover, in countries with more rigid curricula where mathemat-

Distribution of Ph.D. Degrees

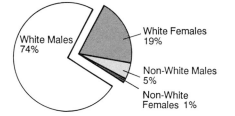

White males earn three of every four doctoral degrees in the mathematical sciences awarded to U.S. citizens.

ics courses are required and students do more homework, gender differences are reduced significantly.

Gender differences in mathematics performance are predominantly due to the accumulated effects of sex-role stereotypes in family, school, and society.

Although American society is committed to equality of opportunity, public attitudes perpetuate stereotypes that "girls can't really do math," that "math is unfeminine," and that "girls don't need much math." As long as these stereotypes persist, young women will continue to drop out prematurely from mathematics education, thereby losing opportunities for future careers. The nation cannot afford this loss, especially in view of the projected shortfall of mathematically trained personnel. We must reduce societal factors that compromise a student's potential to learn mathematics.

Disabled Persons

Mathematics is a field well suited to offering opportunities to disabled individuals. As a mental discipline, mathematics requires only mental acuity for effective performance. Success in mathematics depends neither on physical skills nor on the physical means by which the worker communicates his or her results.

The special opportunities afforded by mathematics for disabled persons apply at all educational levels, in all fields of mathematics, and to all areas of employment. In recent years, the growing use of computers as an aid for disabled people and as a tool for mathematicians provides yet another effective link to enable disabled persons to succeed in mathematics-based careers.

"Although there are barriers for the disabled in mathematics, it is my impression that these barriers are lower in mathematics than in many other fields."

—*I. Richard Savage*

23

Understanding the Universe

Stephen Hawking, a mathematics professor at Cambridge University who holds the chair once occupied by Sir Isaac Newton, has had amyotrophic lateral sclerosis for the last twenty years. One of this century's most brilliant scientists, Hawking uses his mind alone as a tool to explore the secrets of the universe.

M
athematics offers special opportunities as a productive vocation for disabled persons.

Despite the potential of mathematics as a natural vocation for persons with disabilities, far too few recognize or act on this relationship. Many other countries are much more effective in identifying and developing the mathematical talent of disabled persons. With as many as 10 percent of the population disabled in some way, the nation can ill afford continued underrepresentation of disabled persons in mathematical careers.

Graduate Students

Since 1970, the percentage of Americans studying mathematics in graduate schools has declined steadily so that now Americans are frequently a minority in U.S. graduate schools. As in engineering, fewer than half the mathematics doctorates awarded by U.S. universities go to U.S. citizens. Moreover, in the last ten years, the number of U.S. doctorates in the mathematical sciences has dropped by nearly 50 percent.

As Americans drop out of mathematics, international students converge on the United States to study mathematics-based subjects. What our own students see as a burden, students from other countries see as an opportunity. The result is that American graduate schools in mathematically based fields are enrolling ever higher percentages of international students. In mathematics and engineering, nearly half the graduate students are international and over half the graduate degrees now go to international students. This trend is even more pronounced among the best graduate students in the top graduate programs, where as many as three out of four may come from overseas.

As a nation of immigrants, we should welcome the opportunity to be the schoolhouse to the world. Excellent graduate programs—the best in the world—attract the ablest students from around the world, especially from Third World nations where opportunities for advanced study are limited. Many international students remain in the United States to contribute to our research efforts; others return to help raise the mathematical standards of their own countries as ambassadors of American education. Either way, the United States benefits from the opportunity to educate international students; the cause of mathematics is advanced and the insularity of America from the rest of the world is reduced.

T..............................
oo few American students pursue graduate study in the mathematical sciences.

....

Three aspects of international student enrollments do, however, pose serious problems for U.S. mathematics. First, we need to examine why U.S. students are not taking greater advantage of graduate school opportunities in the mathematical sciences. The low percentage of American students in graduate programs is a symptom of grave illness in American pregraduate education. It calls our attention to the obvious—that American mathematics education, especially undergraduate mathematics, is not healthy.

Second, since international students who enroll in U.S. graduate schools typically receive concentrated undergraduate training in mathematics, they compete unevenly in graduate courses with American students who often have had a broad education with less specialization in mathematics. The better preparation of international students discourages many Americans who are trying to embark on career preparation in mathematics, leading to unnecessary dropout from many graduate mathematics programs by capable American students.

Finally, and of most concern to the general public, mathematics departments in universities—more than any other departments—rely on graduate students to teach undergraduates. International graduate students rarely make ideal

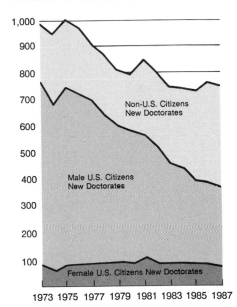

Decline in Mathematics Ph.D.'s

Since 1970, the number of Ph.D. degrees in the mathematical sciences earned by U.S. citizens has declined by nearly 50 percent. The majority of new Ph.D. degrees awarded in U.S. universities now go to foreign citizens.

Undergraduate Instruction

The effect of international students on undergraduate instruction continues well beyond graduate school. In 1987, 40 percent of all full-time assistant professors of mathematics in U.S. doctorate-granting universities received their baccalaureates from non-U.S. universities, as compared with 35 percent for engineering and 20 percent for science overall.

Source: NSF Science Resources.

teachers for American freshmen, for reasons of language, tradition, and background. Good teaching requires experience, empathy with one's students, and the ability to communicate—qualities that are rather uncommon in students only recently arrived in this country. Moreover, students from other nations cannot serve easily as role models for American undergraduates; in many cases, international students find it hard to understand how American students can possibly be the way they are.

Were it not for the large numbers of international students who study and teach in the United States, the state of U.S. mathematics—and science—would be in total disarray. Under current circumstances, most universities have little choice but to employ international graduate students as teaching assistants. Their budgets are not nearly sufficient to staff undergraduate classes with Ph.D.'s; even if they had enough money, the United States does not have enough mathematics Ph.D.'s to fill all college and university positions. As long as universities employ graduate students to teach undergraduates, the best way to improve mathematics instruction for university undergraduates is to recruit more well-qualified American students to graduate study in mathematics.

Supply and Demand

As science and technology become more mathematical, demand by industry for mathematically trained persons increases. Moreover, demand for mathematics teachers increases with demand by industry, since most students who study mathematics do so as background for another subject rather than for majoring in mathematics.

We are now entering a period when the total number of students, after a long decline, is beginning a fifteen-year rise. At the same time, many teachers are nearing retirement, having entered the profession in the heyday of the post-Sputnik era. The consequences of these three factors—rising numbers of students, rising demand for mathematics, and rising retirements of mathematics teachers—will combine to produce very strong demand for mathematics graduates well into the next century. Some projections suggest that the demand for high school mathematics teachers will double in less than ten years.

The potential supply of mathematics teachers is, however, rather weak. For nearly two decades, the number of students receiving degrees in mathematics has been declining, falling roughly 50 percent from its peak in the early 1970's. Although the number of bachelor's degrees earned in the mathematical sciences has begun to rise in recent years, much of this increase represents new joint mathematics-computer science degrees whose holders usually enter computer careers rather than careers in the mathematical sciences.

D emand for mathematics teachers at all levels will exceed the supply of qualified persons throughout the next decade.

Compounding the decline in the number of students selecting degrees in mathematics is the decrease in absolute numbers of Americans in their mid-twenties. The pool from which future mathematicians and mathematics teachers must come is shrinking and will continue to shrink until nearly the end of the century. The number of Americans between 25 and 30 years of age, the age when individuals typically finish their graduate studies, will be 30 percent lower in two decades than it is today.

Many variables influence the national marketplace for mathematics teachers, including regional issues, licensure requirements, degree awards, mathematics course requirements, economic conditions, and competition from private industry. Because so many of these issues are specific to particular states or regions, geographic variation in supply and demand is quite large; surpluses coexist with shortages in a patchwork quilt of very different local markets for mathematics teachers. Despite these variations, however, the overall pattern points to a decade or more of national shortage at every educational level.

Bachelor's Degrees

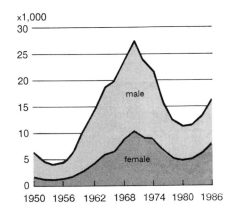

Between 1970 and 1985, the number of undergraduates majoring in mathematics and statistics fell by over 50 percent. In recent years, it has begun to rebound.

Human Resources

Certification vs. Qualification

Data on certification show that most classroom teachers are certified for the simple reason that it is generally illegal for a principal to employ a teacher without proper credentials. Certification comes in many forms—some solid, some flimsy, some permanent, some temporary. Qualification by contemporary standards means much more; it requires solid preparation in the mathematical sciences appropriate to today's curriculum. Even teachers who received substantial preparation twenty years ago may today be unqualified—although fully certified—unless they have kept up with new topics such as statistics and computing that are now important parts of school mathematics.

Even if supply and demand were balanced, mathematics teaching would face a serious shortage of teachers for a different reason: deficit financing of intellectual capital. When demand for mathematics in universities increased sharply during the last decade, most institutions responded either by increasing class size or by hiring underqualified temporary teachers—part-time instructors, graduate assistants, and adjuncts with minimal qualifications and little continuing sense of professional commitment. Even with no changes in student enrollment or faculty retirements, it would take about 10,000 new faculty positions in mathematics just to restore the intellectual and pedagogical vitality of our nation's colleges and universities.

T**oo few mathematics teachers are prepared to teach the mathematics their students need.**

High schools, too, have been filling classroom positions with teachers whose qualifications are substandard—by reassigning teachers with little preparation in mathematics, and none at all in modern mathematics, as demand for mathematics increases. Few elementary school teachers are prepared adequately in mathematics; typically, they take only one of the four courses in mathematics recommended as appropriate preparation for teaching elementary school mathematics.

Of the nation's 200,000 secondary school teachers of mathematics, over half do not meet current professional standards for teaching mathematics. Probably no more than 10 percent of the nation's elementary school teachers meet contemporary standards for their mathematics teaching responsibilities.

Equity and Excellence

Two themes dominate every analysis of American education—the need for equity in opportunity and for excellence in results. Although the goals of equity and excellence sometimes appear to clash, in mathematics education they converge on a single focal point: heightened expectations.

Equity for all students requires a full range of opportunities that can stimulate each person to tap fully his or her interests and capabilities. As students reveal different levels of achievement and different rates of learning, the opportunities and context for the study of mathematics must be continually adjusted to ensure appropriate stimulation and reward for each student. Equity for all requires challenge for all.

Excellence demands that students achieve all that they are capable of accomplishing. National need underscores this demand: our future depends as much on a steady flow of strong and imaginative research leaders as it does on a quantitatively literate work force. Excellence in mathematics education demands results that unfold fully every person's potential.

Many special programs seek to promote equity and excellence. The best of these provide different levels of expectation for students with different levels of need. Such programs educate all students well not by giving them identical assignments but by setting for each child individually appropriate expectations. In such programs, there is no ceiling on a child's aspiration, no perfect grade within easy reach.

E quity for all requires excellence for all; both thrive when expectations are high.

The range of accomplishment in programs devoted to equity and excellence demonstrates to students, teachers, and parents the futility of limited expectations. As educators see the surprising mathematical achievement of students who are stimulated by challenges appropriate to their interests, their entire outlook on appropriate expectations will change. Rising expectations ensure equity and excellence for all.

Options for Excellence

Across the nation, special programs abound to enhance school experience with mathematics, including special statewide mathematics-science high schools, after-school talented youth programs, urban clubs, magnet schools, interscholastic problems contests, summer institutes, and industry internships. All seek to expose young scholars to the challenge and excitement of mathematics. By raising expectations for all, such programs enhance both equity and excellence.

" 'Twice as much, twice as fast, twice as hard' is not an appropriate program for highly talented students."

—*Harvey Keynes*

MATHEMATICS

Mathematics reveals hidden patterns that help us understand the world around us. Now much more than arithmetic and geometry, mathematics today is a diverse discipline that deals with data, measurements, and observations from science; with inference, deduction, and proof; and with mathematical models of natural phenomena, of human behavior, and of social systems.

The cycle from data to deduction to application recurs everywhere mathematics is used, from everyday household tasks such as planning a long automobile trip to major management problems such as scheduling airline traffic or managing investment portfolios. The process of "doing" mathematics is far more than just calculation or deduction; it involves observation of patterns, testing of conjectures, and estimation of results.

As a practical matter, mathematics is a science of pattern and order. Its domain is not molecules or cells, but numbers, chance, form, algorithms, and change. As a science of abstract objects, mathematics relies on logic rather than on observation as its standard of truth, yet employs observation, simulation, and even experimentation as means of discovering truth.

M athematics is a science of pattern and order.

The special role of mathematics in education is a consequence of its universal applicability. The results of mathematics—theorems and theories—are both significant and useful; the best results are also elegant and deep. Through its theorems, mathematics offers science both a foundation of truth and a standard of certainty.

In addition to theorems and theories, mathematics offers distinctive modes of thought which are both versatile and powerful, including modeling, abstraction, optimization, logical analysis, inference from data, and use of symbols. Experience with mathematical modes of thought builds

Mathematical Modes of Thought

Modeling—Representing worldly phenomena by mental constructs, often visual or symbolic, that capture important and useful features.

Optimization—Finding the best solution (least expensive or most efficient) by asking "what if" and exploring all possibilities.

Symbolism—Extending natural language to symbolic representation of abstract concepts in an economical form that makes possible both communication and computation.

Inference—Reasoning from data, from premises, from graphs, from incomplete and inconsistent sources.

Logical Analysis—Seeking implications of premises and searching for first principles to explain observed phenomena.

Abstraction—Singling out for special study certain properties common to many different phenomena.

31

Mathematics

mathematical power—a capacity of mind of increasing value in this technological age that enables one to read critically, to identify fallacies, to detect bias, to assess risk, and to suggest alternatives. Mathematics empowers us to understand better the information-laden world in which we live.

Our Invisible Culture

Mathematics is the invisible culture of our age. Although frequently hidden from public view, mathematical and statistical ideas are embedded in the environment of technology that permeates our lives as citizens. The ideas of mathematics influence the way we live and the way we work on many different levels:

- *Practical*—knowledge that can be put to immediate use in improving basic living standards. The ability to compare loans, to calculate risks, to figure unit prices, to understand scale drawings, and to appreciate the effects of various rates of inflation brings immediate real benefit. This kind of basic applied mathematics is one objective of universal elementary education.

- *Civic*—concepts that enhance understanding of public policy issues. Major public debates on nuclear deterrence, tax rates, and public health frequently center on scientific issues expressed in numeric terms. Inferences drawn from data about crime, projections concerning population growth, and interactions among factors affecting interest rates involve issues with essentially mathematical content. A public afraid or unable to reason with figures is unable to discriminate between rational and reckless claims in public policy. Ideally, secondary school mathematics should help create the "enlightened citizenry" that Thomas Jefferson called the only proper foundation for democracy.

- *Professional*—skill and power necessary to use mathematics as a tool. Science and industry depend increasingly on mathematics as a language of communication and as a methodology of investigation, in applications ranging from theoretical physics to business management. The principal

Back to School

Design a dog house that can be made from a single 4 ft. by 8 ft. sheet of plywood. Make the dog house as large as possible and show how the pieces can be laid out on the plywood before cutting.

M

athematics is a profound and powerful part of human culture.

goal of most college mathematics courses is to provide students with the mathematical prerequisites for their future careers.

- *Leisure*—disposition to enjoy mathematical and logical challenges. The popularity of games of strategy, puzzles, lotteries, and sport wagers reveals a deep vein of amateur mathematics lying just beneath the public's surface indifference. Although few seem eager to admit it, for a lot of people mathematics is really fun.

- *Cultural*—the role of mathematics as a major intellectual tradition, as a subject appreciated as much for its beauty as for its power. The enduring qualities of such abstract concepts as symmetry, proof, and change have been developed through 3,000 years of intellectual effort. They can be understood best as part of the legacy of human culture which we must pass on to future generations. Indeed, it is only when mathematics is viewed as part of the human quest that lay persons can appreciate the esoteric research of twentieth-century mathematics. Like language, religion, and music, mathematics is a universal part of human culture.

These layers of mathematical experience form a matrix of mathematical literacy for the economic and political fabric of society. Although this matrix is generally hidden from public view, it changes regularly in response to challenges arising in science and society. We are now in one of the periods of most active change.

From Abstraction to Application

During the first half of the twentieth century, mathematical growth was stimulated primarily by the power of

"If you want to understand nature, you must be conversant with the language in which nature speaks to us."

—*Richard Feynman*

33

Mathematics

abstraction and deduction, climaxing more than two centuries of effort to extract full benefit from the mathematical principles of physical science formulated by Isaac Newton. Now, as the century closes, the historic alliances of mathematics with science are expanding rapidly; the highly developed legacy of classical mathematical theory is being put to broad and often stunning use in a vast mathematical landscape.

Several particular events triggered periods of explosive growth. The Second World War forced development of many new and powerful methods of applied mathematics. Postwar government investment in mathematics, fueled by Sputnik, accelerated growth in both education and research. Then the development of electronic computing moved mathematics toward an algorithmic perspective even as it provided mathematicians with a powerful tool for exploring patterns and testing conjectures.

At the end of the nineteenth century, the axiomatization of mathematics on a foundation of logic and sets made possible grand theories of algebra, analysis, and topology whose synthesis dominated mathematics research and teaching for the first two thirds of the twentieth century. These traditional areas have now been supplemented by major developments in other mathematical sciences—in number theory, logic, statistics, operations research, probability, computation, geometry, and combinatorics.

In each of these subdisciplines, applications parallel theory. Even the most esoteric and abstract parts of mathematics—number theory and logic, for example—are now used routinely in applications (for example, in computer science and cryptography). Fifty years ago, the leading British mathematician G. H. Hardy could boast that number theory was the most pure and least useful part of mathematics. Today, Hardy's mathematics is studied as an essential prerequisite to many applications, including control of automated systems, data transmission from remote satellites, protection of financial records, and efficient algorithms for computation.

Mathematics is the foundation of science and technology. Without strong mathematics, there can be no strong science.

In 1960, at a time when theoretical physics was the central jewel in the crown of applied mathematics, Eugene Wigner wrote about the "unreasonable effectiveness" of mathematics in the natural sciences: "The miracle of the appropriateness of the language of mathematics for the formulation of the laws of physics is a wonderful gift which we neither understand nor deserve." Theoretical physics has continued to adopt (and occasionally invent) increasingly abstract mathematical models as the foundation for current theories. For example, Lie groups and gauge theories—exotic expressions of symmetry—are fundamental tools in the physicist's search for a unified theory of forces.

During this same period, however, striking applications of mathematics have emerged across the entire landscape of natural, behavioral, and social sciences. All advances in design, control, and efficiency of modern airliners depend on sophisticated mathematical models that simulate performance before prototypes are built. From medical technology (CAT scanners) to economic planning (input/output models of economic behavior), from genetics (decoding of DNA) to geology (locating oil reserves), mathematics has made an indelible imprint on every part of modern science, even as science itself has stimulated the growth of many branches of mathematics.

Applications of one part of mathematics to another—of geometry to analysis, of probability to number theory—provide renewed evidence of the fundamental unity of mathematics. Despite frequent connections among problems in science and mathematics, the constant discovery of new alliances retains a surprising degree of unpredictability and serendipity. Whether planned or unplanned, the cross-fertilization between science and mathematics in problems,

"Equations are just the boring part of mathematics. I attempt to see things in terms of geometry."

—*Stephen Hawking*

35

Mathematics

theories, and concepts has rarely been greater than it is now, in this last quarter of the twentieth century.

Computers

Alongside the growing power of applications of mathematics has been the phenomenal impact of computers. Even mathematicians who never use computers may devote their entire research careers to problems arising from use of computers. Across all parts of mathematics, computers have posed new problems for research, supplied new tools to solve old problems, and introduced new research strategies.

Although the public often views computers as a replacement for mathematics, each is in reality an important tool for the other. Indeed, just as computers afford new opportunities for mathematics, so also it is mathematics that makes computers incredibly effective. Mathematics provides abstract models for natural phenomena as well as algorithms for implementing these models in computer languages. Applications, computers, and mathematics form a tightly coupled system producing results never before possible and ideas never before imagined.

Computers influence mathematics both directly—through stimulation of mathematical research—and indirectly—by their effect on scientific and engineering practice. Computers are now an essential tool in many parts of science and engineering, from weather prediction to protein engineering, from aircraft design to analysis of DNA. In every case, a mathematical model mediates between phenomena of science and simulation provided by the computer.

Scientific computation has become so much a part of the everyday experience of scientific and engineering practice that it can be considered a third fundamental methodology of science—parallel to the more established paradigms of experimental and theoretical science. Computer models of natural, technological, or social systems employ mathematically expressed principles to unfold scenarios under diverse conditions—scenarios that formerly could be studied only through lengthy (and often risky) experiments or prototypes. The methodology of scientific computation embeds mathe-

Myth: As computers become more powerful, the need for mathematics will decline.

Reality: Far from diminishing the importance of mathematics, the pervasive role of computers in science and society contributes to a greatly *increased* role for mathematical ideas, both in research and in civic responsibility. Because of computers, mathematical ideas play central roles in important decisions—on the job, in the home, and in the voting booth.

matical ideas in scientific models of reality as surely as do axiomatic theories or differential equations.

Computer models enable scientists and engineers to reach quickly the mathematical limits permitted by their models. Robotics design, for instance, often encounters limits imposed not by engineering details, but by incomplete understanding of how geometry controls the degrees of freedom of robot motions. Models of weather forecasting consistently reveal uncertainties that suggest intrinsically chaotic behavior. These models also reveal our severely limited knowledge of the mathematical theory of turbulence. Whenever a scientist or engineer uses a computer model to explore the frontiers of knowledge, a new mathematical problem is likely to appear.

Computer models have extended the mathematical sciences into every corner of scientific and engineering practice.

Whereas, traditionally, scientists and engineers who were engaged primarily in experimental research could get along with a small subset of mathematical skills uniquely suited to their field, now even experimentalists need to know a wide range of mathematical methods. Small errors of approximation that are intrinsic to all computer models compound, like interest, with subtle and often devastating results. Only a person who comprehends the mathematics on which computer models are based can use these models effectively and efficiently. Moreover, as a consequence of current limits on computer models, further advances in many areas of scientific and engineering knowledge now depend in essential ways on advances in mathematical research.

The Mathematical Community

Because of its enormous applicability, mathematics is—apart from English—the most widely studied subject in school and college. Present educational practice for mathematics requires approximately 1,500,000 elementary school teachers, 200,000 high school teachers, and 40,000 college and university teachers. Mathematics education takes place in each of 16,000 public school districts, in another 25,000 private schools, in 1,300 community colleges, 1,500 colleges, 400 comprehensive universities, and 200 research universities. Roughly 5,000 mathematicians, principally those on the faculties of the research universities, are engaged in research.

Only half of the nation's students take more than two years of high school-level mathematics; only one quarter take more than three years. That remaining quarter—roughly one million—enter colleges and universities with four years of mathematics. Four years later, about 15,000 students emerge with majors in mathematics. One quarter of these students go on to a master's degree, but only 3 percent (about 400) complete a doctoral degree in the mathematical sciences.

M athematics is the nation's second-largest academic discipline.

Back to School

Two banks are offering car loans with monthly payments of $100. One has an interest rate of 16 percent; the other has a higher rate of 18 percent together with a premium of a free color television (worth $400). If you need a $5,000 loan and would really like the color TV, which bank should you choose?

Just to replace normal retirements and resignations of high school teachers will require about 7,000 to 8,000 new teachers a year, which is half of the expected pool of 15,000 mathematics graduates. Elementary school teachers, in contrast, are drawn primarily from the three quarters of the population who dropped mathematics after two or three courses in high school. For many prospective elementary school teachers, their high school experiences with mathematics were probably not positive. Subsequently, teachers' ambivalent feelings about mathematics are often communicated to children they teach.

In sharp contrast to the eroding conditions of mathematics teaching, one finds enormous vitality and diversity in the breadth of the mathematics profession. Over 25 different organizations in the United States support some facet of professional work in the mathematical sciences. Approximately 50,000 research papers—20,000 by U.S. mathematicians—are published each year in 2,000 mathematics journals around the world. At the school and college level alone, there are over 25 U.S. publications devoted to students and teachers of mathematics. Students and faculty participate in problem-solving activities sponsored by these journals as well as learn about the ways in which current research can relate to curricular change.

This massive system of mathematics education has had no national standards, no global management, and no planned structure—despite the facts that each step in the mathematics curriculum depends in vital ways on what has been accomplished at all earlier stages and that scores of professions depend on skills acquired by students during their study of mathematics. Both because it is so massive and because it is so unstructured, mathematics education in the United States resists change in spite of the many forces that are revolutionizing the nature and role of mathematics.

Undergraduate Mathematics

Undergraduate mathematics is the linchpin for revitalization of mathematics education. Not only do all the sciences depend on strong undergraduate mathematics, but also all students who prepare to teach mathematics acquire attitudes about mathematics, styles of teaching, and knowledge of content from their undergraduate experience. No reform of mathematics education is possible unless it begins with revitalization of undergraduate mathematics in both curriculum and teaching style.

During the last two decades, as undergraduate mathematics enrollments have doubled, the size of the mathematics faculty has increased by less than 30 percent. Workloads are now over 50 percent higher than they were in the post-Sputnik years and are typically among the highest on many campuses. Resources generated by the vigorous demand for undergraduate mathematics are rarely used to improve un-

"Between now and the year 2000, for the first time in history, a majority of all new jobs will require postsecondary education."

—*Workforce 2000*

39

Mathematics

A Pipeline to Science

The undergraduate mathematics major not only prepares students for graduate study in mathematics, but also for many other sciences. Indeed, nearly twice as many mathematics majors go on to receive a Ph.D. in another scientific field rather than in the mathematical sciences themselves.

dergraduate mathematics teaching. To administrators worried about tight budgets, mathematics departments are often the best bargains on campus, but to students seeking stimulation and opportunity, mathematics departments are often the Rip Van Winkle of the academic community.

Reform of undergraduate mathematics is the key to revitalizing mathematics education.

During these same two decades, both the opportunity and the need for vital innovative mathematics instruction have increased substantially. The subject moves on, yet the curriculum is stagnant. Only a minority of the nation's collegiate faculty maintains a program of significant professional activity. Even fewer are regularly engaged in mathematical research, but these few sustain a research enterprise that is the best in the world. Unfortunately, those who are most professionally active rarely teach any undergraduate course related to their scholarly work as mathematicians. Mathematicians seldom teach what they think about—and rarely think deeply about what they teach.

Departments of mathematics in colleges and universities serve several different constituencies: general education, teacher education, client departments, and future mathematicians. Very few departments have the intellectual and financial resources to meet well the needs of all these frequently conflicting groups. Worse still, most departments fail to meet the needs of *any* of these constituencies with energy, effectiveness, or distinction.

Since almost everyone who teaches mathematics is educated in our colleges and universities, many issues facing mathematics education hinge on revitalization of undergraduate mathematics. But critical curricular review and revitalization take time, energy, and commitment—essential ingredients that have been stripped from the mathematics faculty by two decades of continuous deficits. Rewards of promotion and tenure follow research, not curricular reform;

neither institutions of higher education nor the professional community of mathematicians encourages faculty to devote time and energy to revitalization of undergraduate mathematics.

To improve mathematics education, we must restore integrity to undergraduate mathematics. This challenge provides a great opportunity. With approximately 50 percent of school teachers leaving every seven years, it is feasible to make significant changes in the way school mathematics is taught simply by transforming undergraduate mathematics to reflect the new expectations for mathematics. Undergraduate mathematics is the bridge between research and schools and holds the power of reform in mathematics education.

CURRICULUM

Mathematics is one way we make sense of things. It enables us to perceive patterns, to comprehend data, and to reason carefully. Truth and beauty, utility and application frame the study of mathematics like the muses of Greek theater. Together, they define mathematical power, the objective of mathematics education.

The transformation of mathematics from a core of abstract studies to a powerful family of mathematical sciences is reflected poorly, often not at all, by the traditional mathematics curriculum. One can hardly blame students for not becoming interested in mathematics if they rarely see evidence of its full power and richness.

. . . .

Mathematics curricula at all levels must introduce more of the breadth and power of the mathematical sciences.

. . . .

As mathematics is more than calculation, so education in mathematics must be more than mastery of arithmetic. Geometry, chance, and change are as important as numbers in achieving mathematical power. Even more important is a comprehensive flexible view that embodies the intrinsic unity of mathematics: estimation supplements calculation; heuristics aid algorithms; experience balances innovation. To prepare students to use mathematics in the twenty-first century, today's curriculum must invoke the full spectrum of the mathematical sciences.

Philosophy

Virtually all young children like mathematics. They do mathematics naturally, discovering patterns and making conjectures based on observation. Natural curiosity is a powerful teacher, especially for mathematics.

Curriculum

Unfortunately, as children become socialized by school and society, they begin to view mathematics as a rigid system of externally dictated rules governed by standards of accuracy, speed, and memory. Their view of mathematics shifts gradually from enthusiasm to apprehension, from confidence to fear. Eventually, most students leave mathematics under duress, convinced that only geniuses can learn it. Later, as parents, they pass this conviction on to their children. Some even become teachers and convey this attitude to their students.

Doing mathematics is much like writing. In each, the final product must express good ideas clearly and correctly, but the ideas must be present before the expression can take form. Good ideas poorly expressed can be revised to improve their form; empty ideas well expressed are not worth revising. A mathematics curriculum that emphasizes computation and rules is like a writing curriculum that emphasizes grammar and spelling; both put the cart before the horse.

Excessive emphasis on mechanics of mathematics not only inhibits learning, but also leads to widespread misconceptions among the public concerning strengths and limitations of mathematical methods. Because early school experiences suggest that all mathematics problems have a single correct answer, the public—to its great risk—tends to believe uncritically any expert who employs mathematical arguments. Such a misconception can lead to disastrous consequences when naive mathematical modeling is used as the basis for economic, military, or social planning. Too few of those who use mathematical models are well enough prepared to appreciate the limitations of the models they use.

Mathematics instruction must not reinforce the common impression that the only problems amenable to mathematical analysis are those that have unique correct answers. Even more, it must not leave the impression that mathematical ideas are the product of authority or wizardry. Mathematics is a natural mode of human thought, better suited to certain types of problems than to others, yet always subject to confirmation and checking with other types of analyses. There is no place in a proper curriculum for mindless mimicry mathematics.

S......................................elf-confidence built on success is the most important objective of the mathematics curriculum.

....

The ability of individuals to cope with mathematics wherever it arises in their later lives—whether as wage-earners, parents, or citizens—depends on the attitudes toward mathematics conveyed in school and college classes. Above all, mathematics curricula must avoid leaving a legacy of misunderstanding, apprehension, and fear.

Standards

Independence is the hallmark of U.S. education. Educational policy is set not by the U.S. Department of Education, but by fifty states and thousands of independent school districts. Local control of education is embedded in the American body politic as deeply as anything, a legacy of constitutional authority that reserves to the states all matters not expressly granted to the federal government.

Yet this independence is largely a myth, especially for mathematics education. Effective control comes not from Washington, but from invisible local or state committees that approve textbooks and from anonymous officials who select standardized tests. Few facts stand undisputed in educational research, but the dependence of teachers on textbooks and of students on tests is as firm a finding as exists in this amorphous discipline; especially in mathematics, teachers teach only what is in the textbook and students learn only what will be on the test.

In practice, although not in law, we have a national curriculum in mathematics education. It is an "underachieving" curriculum that follows a spiral of almost constant radius, reviewing each year so much of the past that little new learning takes place. Some states (for example, California, Texas, Wisconsin, and New York) have recently promulgated new standards for mathematics education, often with surprising

Myth: What was good enough for me is good enough for my child.

Reality: Today's world is more mathematical than yesterday's, and tomorrow's world will be more mathematical than today's. As computers increase in power, some parts of mathematics become less important while other parts become more important. While arithmetic proficiency may have been "good enough" for many in the middle of the century, anyone whose mathematical skills are limited to computation has little to offer today's society that is not done better by an inexpensive machine.

Curriculum

consequences. In California, new standards led to initial rejection of *all* mathematics textbook series submitted for authorized adoption. California wanted to stress as emphatically as possible that, in the future, mathematics textbooks must be designed to develop student capabilities to address and solve complex, subtle, and unpredictable problems.

America needs to reach consensus on national standards for school mathematics.

We must judge schools not by remembrances of things past, but by necessary expectations for the future. Students must learn not only arithmetic, but also estimation, measurement, geometry, optimization, statistics, and probability— all of the ways in which mathematics occurs in everyday life. In the process, they must gain confidence in their ability to communicate and reason about mathematics; they should become mathematical problem-solvers.

Elementary Education

Elementary school is where children learn the mathematical skills needed for daily life. Formerly, shopkeeper arithmetic was an adequate objective since, for most people, mathematics in daily life required little more than arithmetic.

This is no longer true. Calculators now do most of the arithmetic needed for daily life, while a technology-dominated society requires that everyone have a good grasp of chance, of reasoning, of form, and of pattern. While the goal of elementary education has not changed, the mathematical objectives appropriate to this goal are very different now from what they were half a century ago.

The major objective of elementary school mathematics should be to develop number sense. Like common sense,

Myth: Arithmetic is the major goal of elementary school mathematics.

Reality: Number sense builds on arithmetic as words build on the alphabet. Numbers arise in measurement, in chance, in data, and in geometry, as well as in arithmetic. Mathematics in elementary school should weave all these threads together to create in children a robust sense of numbers.

46

number sense produces good and useful results with the least amount of effort. It is not mindlessly mechanical, but flexible and synthetic in attitude. It evolves from concrete experience and takes shape in oral, written, and symbolic expression. Links to geometry, to chance, and to calculation should reinforce formal arithmetic experience to produce multiple mental images of quantitative phenomena.

Developing number sense will move children (and teachers) beyond narrow concern for school-certified algorithms for arithmetic. Even in the absence of calculators, neither children nor adults make much use of the specific arithmetic techniques taught in school. School children do, however, need to learn how to use mathematics for common tasks—making change, measuring quantities (food, lumber, fabric), planning schedules, estimating chances—but the particular means that they use must be appropriate to the task. They need to learn not only how to estimate and calculate, but also how to decide whether to estimate or calculate. Good number sense includes common sense about how to find an answer as well as a range of choices of methods.

A...ppropriate use of calculators enhances children's understanding and mastery of arithmetic.

....

Using calculators intelligently is an integral part of number sense. Children should use calculators throughout their school work, just as adults use calculators throughout their lives. More important, children must learn when to use them and when not to do so. They must learn from experience with calculators when to estimate and when to seek an exact answer; how to estimate answers to verify the plausibility of calculator results; and how to solve modest problems mentally when neither pencil nor calculator is convenient.

Calculators create whole new opportunities for ordering the curriculum and for integrating mathematics into science.

Back to School
"Target Addition" is a calculator game that reinforces mental arithmetic. Two children with a calculator agree on a target number such as 21. They take turns adding a number from 1 to 5 into the memory. The goal is to make the memory number match the target number.

Curriculum

No longer need teachers be constrained by the artificial restriction to numbers that children know how to employ in the paper-and-pencil algorithms of arithmetic. Decimals can be introduced much earlier since they arise naturally on the calculator. Real measurements from science experiments can be used in mathematics lessons because the calculator will be able to add or multiply the data even if the children have not yet learned how. They may learn first what addition and multiplication mean and when to use them, and only later how to perform these operations manually in all possible cases.

Elementary school mathematics should reinforce a child's natural curiosity about patterns. Children must be encouraged to perceive mathematics in the world around them. Shapes, numbers, chance—the foundations of geometry, arithmetic, probability—will emerge from careful guided observation. Science study will lead naturally to mathematics, following the paradigm of data, deduction, and observation.

Many adults fear that early introduction of calculators will prevent children from learning basic arithmetic "properly," as their parents learned it. The experiences of many schools during the last fifteen years show that this fear is unfounded. Students who use calculators learn traditional arithmetic as well as those who do not use calculators and emerge from elementary school with better problem-solving skills and much better attitudes about mathematics. Although mindless calculation can be as destructive as mindless arithmetic, proper use of calculators can stimulate growth of a realistic and productive number sense in each child.

Secondary Education

Secondary education is where students begin to learn the mathematics they will need for careers as well as the mathematics required for effective citizenship. Whereas, traditionally, secondary school has been characterized by the introduction of algebra as an extension of arithmetic, contemporary society requires much greater breadth from secondary school mathematics.

The focus of the secondary school curriculum remains—as it should—on the transition from concrete to conceptual mathematics. As students' understanding moves from numbers to variables, from description to proof, from special cases to general equations, they learn the power of mathematical symbols. In a very real sense, the major objective of secondary school mathematics is to develop symbol sense.

All students need to leave secondary school well prepared mathematically for leading intelligent lives as productive citizens—since even many of those who go on to higher education will take little or no further mathematics. High school graduates need to know enough about chance to understand health and environmental risks; enough about change and variability to understand investments; enough about data and experiments to understand the grounds for scientific conclusions; enough about representation to interpret graphs; and enough about the nature of mathematics to be supportive parents to their children who will learn aspects of mathematics that their parents never studied.

Students who enter the work force directly from high school will be expected to be able to read documents replete with technical language—computer guides, shop manuals, financial reports. They need to be able to comprehend three-dimensional images (assembly diagrams) and logically intricate instructions (tax code); they need to be able to read symbol-laden text (computer manuals) and to plan complex systems (purchasing property). They need enough mathematics and enough confidence to be able to learn what they need as they need it.

A.................................
ll high school students should study a common core of broadly useful mathematics.

....

Typically, secondary school mathematics curricula are dominated by a philosophy of preparation for college calculus. Few natural applications emerge from secondary school

Back to School

Investigate the relation between automobile mileage and age by gathering data from cars in the school parking lot.

AIDS Tests

How is it possible for an AIDS test that is 95 percent accurate to be misleading 90 percent of the time when used in mass testing? Issues such as this are central to public policy, yet require a basic knowledge of probability to be understood properly.

Curriculum

mathematics since the traditional topics are merely tools for the applications of calculus. Even worse, students rarely learn mathematics appropriate to enlightened citizenship or to the needs of the workplace.

These deficiencies are not inherent in secondary school mathematics, but historical accidents arising from the teleological influence of calculus. New mathematics with broader applications can offer much greater appeal to all students. Instead of tracking students by curricular objective (for example, commercial, general, or precollege), school mathematics should provide for all students a core of mainstream mathematics in which different student groups are distinguished not by curricular goals, but only by speed, depth, and approach.

For students planning to enter college, still more is needed: thorough grounding in mathematical methods required for calculus, statistics, and computer science. As these collegiate subjects change in response to the impact of computers, the prerequisites will shift away from formal algebra to more integrative, problem-solving approaches. Versatility, confidence, experience, reasoning, and communication about mathematics are skills that will be valued as prerequisites to college mathematics.

Myth: The primary goal of mathematics education is to educate mathematicians.

Reality: School mathematics is part of universal education. Three of every four college majors require students to study college-level mathematics. To cope with a technological age, all students should study mathematics every year they are in school.

A..................................
ll students should study mathematics every year they are in school.
....

The gradual mathematization of society has increased continuously the amount of mathematics that students must learn. Universal elementary education has been replaced, for all practical purposes, by universal secondary education. As a consequence, students' study of mathematics must continue throughout secondary school.

Higher Education

Most students who enter postsecondary education must study further mathematics, either as part of a general degree requirement or as a prerequisite to their particular course of study. In this regard, vocational-technical institutes, community colleges, continuing education, and adult education programs are no different from four-year colleges and universities. Most courses of study have some kind of mathematical prerequisite and most students find that they need additional study of mathematics to meet these prerequisites.

Over three quarters of the degree programs at most universities require courses in calculus, discrete mathematics, statistics, or other comparable mathematics. These subjects are required because they introduce students to functions, to relations among variables. The language of change and chance is conveyed by the symbolism of functions. College students need this level of mathematical literacy in order to understand with precision the mathematical ideas that form the foundations for science, business, and engineering courses.

Learning mathematics entails a gradual progression from the concrete to the abstract, from the specific to the general. Numbers lead to symbols, to names for variables; relations among symbols lead to functions, to the links among objects expressed in symbols. If it does nothing else, undergraduate mathematics should help students develop function sense—a familiarity with expressing relations among variables.

Nine of every ten mathematics course enrollments in higher education are in elementary calculus, in elementary statistics, or in courses that are prerequisites to these subjects. Prerequisite courses are normal parts of the secondary school curriculum and should, if at all possible, be studied there rather than in college. Elementary statistics is not often taught in secondary schools today, but should become a regular part of secondary school mathematics. Calculus, taught both in high school and in college, is the principal gateway through which most students must pass if they are to prepare for mathematics-based careers.

Although discrete mathematics and statistics provide nec-

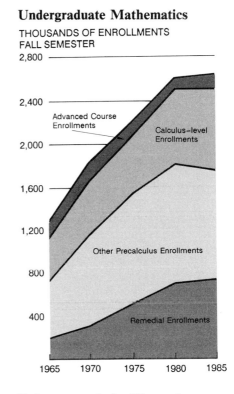

Undergraduate Mathematics

THOUSANDS OF ENROLLMENTS
FALL SEMESTER

Each term, nearly 3 million students enroll in postsecondary mathematics courses. About 60 percent study elementary mathematics and statistics below the level of calculus, while 30 percent take calculus-level courses. The remaining 10 percent study higher (post-calculus) mathematics.

51

Curriculum

Symbolic Computer Systems

As calculators have surpassed human capacity for arithmetic calculations, so now are symbolic computer packages overtaking human ability to carry out the calculations of calculus. Until recently, computers could only operate numerically (with rounded numbers) and graphically (with visual approximations). But now they can operate *symbolically* just as people do, solving equations in terms of x and y just as we teach students in school mathematics. Symbolic computer systems compel fundamental rethinking of what we teach and how we teach it.

essary foundations for computer, engineering, and social sciences, calculus remains the archetype of higher mathematics. It is a powerful and elegant example of the mathematical method, leading both to major applications and to major theories. The language of calculus has spread to all scientific fields; the insight it conveys about the nature of change is something that no educated person can afford to be without.

Unfortunately, calculus as presently taught has little in common with the way calculus is used. Many students who enroll never complete the course; many of those who do finish learn little beyond a series of memorized techniques now more commonly performed by computers. Because of the central importance of calculus for all scientific study and research, the National Science Foundation has launched an initiative to improve instruction in calculus, which is now studied by nearly one million students every year.

S . . . .
uccessful calculus is essential to healthy mathematics and science.
. . . .

The quality of calculus instruction is a barometer of mathematics education. Since preparation for calculus has been the organizing principle of high school mathematics, calculus receives the inheritance of school practice. Changes in calculus reverberate throughout secondary school curricula, just as changes in school mathematics are magnified by the challenge of calculus. Although other courses need improving as much as calculus, and although many courses are as important or as practical, the unique position of calculus as the gateway from school to college mathematics imposes on it a special burden to be attractive, compelling, and intellectually stimulating.

For the past two decades, enrollments in mathematics service courses in colleges and universities have been rising, yet throughout most of that period the number of mathematics majors has been declining. Part of this paradox is due to career competition from attractive disciplines that are new users of mathematics, notably computer science, economics, and now, increasingly, biology. But another part of the problem lies with the mathematics major itself, which in many institutions has continued a narrow focus on graduate school preparation, ignoring the many students who might (and should) major in mathematics as a versatile preparation for careers in other disciplines.

U.................................ndergraduate mathematics provides a powerful platform for careers in many fields.

....

Building and sustaining a mathematics major with broad appeal require commitment to integrity in the undergraduate program:

- Freshman and sophomore courses (especially calculus and linear algebra) should be taught by the most able instructors who can motivate students to study mathematics.

- Introductory courses must be taught in a manner that reflects the era in which we live, making full use of computers as an integral tool for instruction and for mathematics.

- Upper-division offerings should be designed to represent broadly the several mathematical sciences, introducing students in appropriate ways to applications, computing, modeling, and modern topics.

- Diverse opportunities outside formal classroom work should be provided so that students can engage in mathematics through projects, research, teaching, problem-solving, or independent study.

Broad undergraduate mathematics programs will attract more students to extended study of mathematics, will offer these students appealing opportunities to explore mathematics applicable to many fields, and will engage good students in exploring and learning mathematics on their own. Such

Continuing Education

Almost as many persons study mathematics outside traditional school structures as inside them. Whereas mathematics curricula have been conceived in the traditional structure of continuous grade-level education from childhood to early adulthood, today much mathematics is studied by older adults. Some large businesses actually operate mini-school districts just for the continuing education of employees; many universities and colleges—especially community colleges—attract large numbers of adults both to regular degree programs and to special short courses for professional growth or cultural enrichment. Every issue of purpose, quality, and effectiveness concerning traditional mathematics education also affects continuing mathematics education. The need for renewal in the nontraditional forums is just as urgent as it is within the walls of traditional schools.

an approach, while intended as a foundation for students in many different majors, will inevitably attract good students to careers in mathematics.

Demographic data and degree trends show that it is vitally important for undergraduate mathematics departments to offer effective, broad-based curricula. The United States needs more American graduate students in the mathematical sciences; more mathematics graduates who can teach in secondary schools; and more students with better preparation in mathematics entering graduate programs in science and engineering. Redressing the serious shortage of mathematically educated college graduates is a significant and urgent challenge to our mathematics faculties.

TEACHING

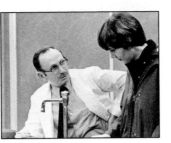

...learning through involvement

There is little we do in America that is more important than teaching. Effective teaching of mathematics requires appropriate pedagogical and mathematical foundations, but thrives only in an environment of trust which encourages leadership and innovation. In short, teaching must become more professional.

Under current conditions, most school teachers face nearly insurmountable obstacles. Lacking freedom to establish fully either ends or means, teachers rarely have the opportunity to exercise truly professional responsibilities. What emerges, often, are foreshortened ideals and shattered dreams.

Evidence from many sources shows that the least effective mode for mathematics learning is the one that prevails in most of America's classrooms: lecturing and listening. Despite daily homework, for most students and most teachers mathematics continues to be primarily a passive activity: teachers prescribe; students transcribe. Students simply do not retain for long what they learn by imitation from lectures, worksheets, or routine homework. Presentation and repetition help students do well on standardized tests and lower-order skills, but they are generally ineffective as teaching strategies for long-term learning, for higher-order thinking, and for versatile problem-solving.

Teachers, however, almost always present mathematics as an established doctrine to be learned just as it was taught. This "broadcast" metaphor for learning leads students to expect that mathematics is about right answers rather than about clear creative thinking. In the early grades, arithmetic becomes the stalking horse for this authoritarian model of learning, sowing seeds of expectation that dominate student attitudes all the way through college.

Understanding Mathematics

Many students master the formalisms of mathematics without, at first, any real understanding. Some go on to achieve a retrospective understanding after they have reached a more advanced vantage point. Surprisingly, many mathematicians and scientists recall that their own educa-

Myth: Learning mathematics means mastering an immutable set of basic skills.

Reality: Skills are to mathematics what scales are to music or spelling is to writing. The objective of learning is to write, to play music, or to solve problems—not just to master skills. Practice with skills is just one of many strategies used by good teachers to help students achieve the broader goals of learning.

57

Teaching

Back to School

A table of data gives information on stopping distances for several cars in terms of speed, weight, and types of brakes (drum, disc, antilock). The information includes both reaction time distance as well as braking distance. Develop a model for these data in terms of graphs, equations, or computer programs that would enable one to predict how other cars would handle under similar circumstances. Compare what the model predicts with the advice given in driver education courses.

tion fits this model; rarely is anything learned well until it is revisited from a more advanced perspective.

The vast majority of students never move beyond formal knowledge since they do not persist in subsequent work to reach the point where the veil of confusion is lifted. (Those who do persist are likely to be the ones who subsequently go on to careers in science.) Present educational practice in the United States offers students only one path to understanding—a long, dimly lit journey through a mountain of meaningless manipulations, with the reward of power and understanding available only to those who complete the journey.

P . . . .
resent educational practice offers mathematics students only a dim light at the end of a very long tunnel.

. . . .

Most students do not find the light at the end of the tunnel sufficient to illuminate their journey through the mathematics curriculum. Far too many abandon their effort before receiving any benefit from the power of retrospective understanding. To improve mathematics education for all students, we need to expand teaching practices that engage and motivate students as they struggle with their own learning. In addition to beckoning with the light of future understanding at the end of the tunnel, we need even more to increase illumination in the interior of the tunnel.

Learning Mathematics

In reality, no one can *teach* mathematics. Effective teachers are those who can stimulate students to *learn* mathematics. Educational research offers compelling evidence that students learn mathematics well only when they *construct* their own mathematical understanding. To understand what they learn, they must enact for themselves verbs that permeate the mathematics curriculum: "examine," "represent," "transform," "solve," "apply," "prove," "communicate." This happens most readily when students work in groups, engage in discussion, make presentations, and in other ways take charge of their own learning.

All students engage in a great deal of invention as they learn mathematics; they impose their own interpretation on what is presented to create a theory that makes sense to them. Students do not learn simply a subset of what they have been shown. Instead, they use new information to modify their prior beliefs. As a consequence, each student's knowledge of mathematics is uniquely personal.

S......................................
tudents retain best the mathematics that they learn by processes of internal construction and experience.

....

Evidence that students construct a hierarchy of understanding through processes of assimilation and accommodation with prior belief is not new; hints can be found in the work of Piaget over fifty years ago. Insights from contemporary cognitive science help confirm these earlier observations by establishing a theoretical framework based on evidence from many fields of study.

Engaging Students

No teaching can be effective if it does not respond to students' prior ideas. Teachers need to listen as much as they need to speak. They need to resist the temptation to control classroom ideas so that students can gain a sense of ownership over what they are learning. Doing this requires genuine give-and-take in the mathematics classroom, both among students and between students and teachers. The

Myth: Students learn by remembering what they are taught.

Reality: Students construct meaning as they learn mathematics. They use what they are taught to modify their prior beliefs and behavior, not simply to record and store what they are told. It is students' acts of construction and invention that build their mathematical power and enable them to solve problems they have never seen before.

Teaching

Robust Arithmetic

How do you add up long lists of numbers? A dozen different people do it in a dozen different ways—top down, bottom up, grouping by tens, bunching, and various mixtures. There is no single correct method.

best way to develop effective logical thinking is to encourage open discussion and honest criticism of ideas.

Clear presentations by themselves are inadequate to replace existing misconceptions with correct ideas. What students have constructed for themselves, however inadequate it may be, is often too deeply ingrained to be dislodged with a lecture followed by a few exercises. To change beliefs, students need to have a stake in the outcome.

Honest questions by teachers are rare in mathematics classrooms. Most teachers ask rhetorical questions because they are not so much interested in what students really think as in whether they know the right answer. Soon, students are plaguing teachers with their own rhetorical question: "Can't you just tell me the answer?"

When students explore mathematics on their own, they construct strategies that bear little resemblance to the canonical examples presented in standard textbooks. Just as children need the opportunity to learn from mistakes, so students need an environment for learning mathematics that provides generous room for trial and error. In the long run, it is not the memorization of mathematical skills that is particularly important—without constant use, skills fade rapidly—but the confidence that one knows how to find and use mathematical tools whenever they become necessary. There is no way to build this confidence except through the process of creating, constructing, and discovering mathematics.

Mathematics teachers must involve students in their own learning.

Classes in which students are told how to solve a quadratic equation and then assigned a dozen homework problems to learn the approved method will rarely stimulate much lasting mathematical knowledge. Far better is an approach in which students encounter such equations in a natural context; explore several approaches to solutions, including estimation, graphs, computers, and algebra; then compare various approaches and argue about their merits. Of course, classes such as this where active learning is a way of life require more time and energy on the part of both teachers and students than either is accustomed to giving under present conditions.

Teachers' roles should include those of consultant, moderator, and interlocutor, not just presenter and authority. Classroom activities must encourage students to express *their* approaches, both orally and in writing. Students must engage mathematics as a human activity; they must learn to work cooperatively in small teams to solve problems as well as to argue convincingly for their approach amid conflicting ideas and strategies.

There is a price to pay for less directive strategies of teaching. In many cases, greater instructional effort may be required. In those parts of the curriculum where mathematics directly serves another discipline (for example, engineering), students may not march through the required curriculum at the expected rate. In the long run, however, less teaching will yield more learning. As students begin to take responsibility for their own work, they will learn *how* to learn as well as *what* to learn.

Impact of Computers

Calculators and computers compel reexamination of priorities for mathematics education. How many adults, whether store clerks or bookkeepers, still do long division (or even long multiplication) by paper and pencil? How many scientists or engineers use paper-and-pencil methods to carry out their scientific calculations? Who would trust a bank that kept its records in ledgerbooks?

Those who use mathematics in the workplace—accountants, engineers, scientists—rarely use paper-and-pencil procedures any more, certainly not for significant or complex analyses. Electronic spreadsheets, numerical analysis packages, symbolic computer systems, and sophisticated com-

Calculators vs. Computers
Polls show that the public generally thinks that, in mathematics education, calculators are bad while computers are good. People believe that calculators will prevent children from mastering arithmetic, an important burden which their parents remember bearing with courage and pride. Computers, on the other hand, are not perceived as shortcuts to undermine school traditions, but as new tools necessary to society that children who understand mathematics must learn to use. What the public fails to recognize is that both calculators and computers are equally essential to mathematics education and have equal potential for wise use or for abuse.

Teaching

puter graphics have become the power tools of mathematics in industry. Even research mathematicians now use computers to aid exploration, conjecture, and proof.

In spite of the intimate intellectual link between mathematics and computing, school mathematics has responded hardly at all to curricular changes implied by the computer revolution. Curricula, texts, tests, and teaching habits—but not the students—are all products of the precomputer age. Little could be worse for mathematics education than an environment in which schools hold students back from learning what they find natural.

It is true, as many say, that we are not sure how best to teach mathematics with computers. Nevertheless, despite risks of venturing into unfamiliar territory, society has much to gain from the increasing role of calculators and computers in mathematics education:

- School mathematics can become more like the mathematics people actually use, both on the job and in scientific applications. By using machines to expedite calculations, students can experience mathematics as it really is—as a tentative exploratory discipline in which risks and failures yield clues to success.

- Weakness in algebraic skills need no longer prevent students from understanding ideas in more advanced mathematics. Just as computerized spelling checkers permit writers to express ideas without the psychological block of terrible spelling, so will the new calculators enable motivated students who are weak in algebra or trigonometry to persevere in calculus or statistics. Calculators in the classroom can help make higher mathematics more accessible.

- Mathematics learning can become more active and dynamic, hence more effective. By carrying much of the computational burden of mathematics homework, calculators and computers enable students to explore a wider variety of examples; to witness the dynamic nature of mathematical processes; to engage realistic applications using typical—not oversimplified—data; and to focus on important concepts rather than routine calculation.

- Students can explore mathematics on their own, to ask and answer countless "what if" questions. Although calculators

Tomorrow's Computers

Even as teachers struggle to adapt yesterday's curriculum to today's computers, industrial leaders are designing tomorrow's technology. Multimegabyte memory and gigabyte storage support unprecedented graphics, unleashing potential for interactive textbooks, remote classrooms, and integrated learning environments. As today's computer visions become tomorrow's verities, they will revolutionize the way mathematics is practiced and the way it is learned.

and computers will not necessarily cause students to think for themselves, they can provide an environment in which student-generated mathematical ideas can thrive.

- Time invested in mathematics study can build long-lasting intuition and insight, not just short-lived strategies for calculation. Innovative instruction based on a new symbiosis of machine calculation and human thinking can shift the balance of learning toward understanding, insight, and mathematical intuition.

Ten years ago, arithmetic fell to the power of inexpensive hand calculators; five years ago, scientific calculators offered at the touch of a button more sophisticated numerical mathematics than most students knew anything about. Today's calculators can do a large fraction of all techniques taught in the first two years of college mathematics. Tomorrow's calculators will do what computers do today.

Priorities for mathematics education must change to reflect the way computers are used in mathematics.

The ready availability of versatile calculators and computers establishes new ground rules for mathematics education. Template exercises and mimicry mathematics—the staple diet of today's texts—will diminish under the assault of machines that specialize in mimicry. Instructors will be forced to change their approach and their assignments. It will no longer do for teachers to teach as they were taught in the paper-and-pencil era.

Education of Teachers

Mathematics is taught in every grade throughout the entire thirteen years of school, K–12; consistent growth in skills,

Myth: The way to improve students' mathematical performance is to stress the basics.

Reality: Basics from the past, especially manual arithmetic, are of less value today than yesterday—except to score well on tests of basic skills. Today's students need to learn *when* to use mathematics as much as they need to learn *how* to use it. Basic skills for the twenty-first century include more than just manual mathematics.

Teaching

Back to School

Record the height and weight of everyone in your class and see what relationship you can determine. Do age or sex help make the relationship clear?

maturity, and understanding is essential as students move from one level to the next. As a chain that breaks at its weakest link, mathematics instruction is especially vulnerable to weakness in any grade or course. For this reason, the preparation of mathematics teachers is a crucial factor in revitalizing curricular practice.

Too often, elementary teachers take only one course in mathematics, approaching it with trepidation and leaving it with relief. Such experiences leave many elementary teachers totally unprepared to inspire children with confidence in their own mathematical abilities. What is worse, experienced elementary teachers often move up to middle grades (because of imbalance in enrollments) without learning any more mathematics.

Those who would teach mathematics need to learn contemporary mathematics appropriate to the grades they will teach, in a style consistent with the way in which they will be expected to teach. They also need to learn how students learn—what we know from research (not much, but important), and what we do not know (a great deal). They need to learn science (including technology, business, and social science) so that they can teach mathematics in the contexts where it arises most naturally—in measurement, graphs, prediction, decisions, and data analysis. And they need to learn the history of mathematics and its impact on society, for it is only through history that teachers will come to know that mathematics changes and to see the differences between contemporary and ancient mathematics.

The United States is one of the few countries in the world that continues to pretend—despite substantial evidence to the contrary—that elementary school teachers are able to teach all subjects equally well. It is time that we identify a cadre of teachers with special interests in mathematics and science who would be well prepared to teach young children both mathematics and science in an integrated, discovery-based environment.

The United States must create a tradition of elementary school specialists to teach mathematics and science.

Many models for mathematics specialists are possible, most of which are in place in different school districts today. Implementation can range from paired classes—one teacher for language arts, the other for mathematics and science—to certified specialists who lead curricular development and assist regular classroom teachers. Many teachers already have the interest, experience, and enthusiasm for such positions; others could qualify through special summer institutes.

To encourage more widespread adoption of diverse patterns for mathematics specialists, states must alter certification requirements to encourage these new models. Then universities must implement new courses with open constructive instructors so that prospective school teachers can grow in confidence as a result of their university study of mathematics. The content of the special mathematics courses for prospective elementary and middle school teachers—those who do not undertake a standard mathematics major—must be infused by examples of mathematics in the world that the child sees (sports, architecture, house, and home), examples that illustrate change, quantity, shape, chance, and dimension.

Teachers themselves need experience in doing mathematics—in exploring, guessing, testing, estimating, arguing, and proving—in order to develop confidence that they can respond constructively to unexpected conjectures that emerge as students follow their own paths in approaching mathematical problems. Too often, mathematics teachers are afraid that someone will ask a question that they cannot answer. Insecurity breeds rigidity, the antithesis of mathematical power.

Since teachers teach much as they were taught, university courses for prospective teachers must exemplify the highest standards for instruction. However, most mathematics that

Back to School

You have 10 items in your grocery cart. Six people are waiting in the express lane (10 items or less); one person is waiting in lane 1 and two people are waiting in lane 3. The other lanes are closed. What additional information do you need to know in order to determine which lane to join?

teachers have studied has been presented only in the authoritarian framework of Moses coming down from Mt. Sinai. Very few teachers have had the experience of constructing for themselves any of the mathematics that they are asked to teach, of listening to students who are developing their own mathematical understandings, or of guiding students to their own discovery of mathematical insights.

Prospective teachers should learn mathematics in a manner that encourages active engagement with mathematical ideas.

All students, and especially prospective teachers, should learn mathematics as a process of constructing and interpreting patterns, of discovering strategies for solving problems, and of exploring the beauty and applications of mathematics. Above all, courses taken by prospective teachers must create in these teachers confidence in their own abilities to help students discover richness and excitement in mathematics.

Resources

Textbooks and their ancillary products (worksheets, homework exercises, testbanks) dominate mathematics teaching at all levels, from primary school through college. In no other subject do students operate so close to a single prescribed text; neither library work nor laboratory work, neither term papers nor special projects are common parts of mathematics instruction. Classroom mathematics is the study of set texts and set problems that rarely have any parallel either in the world of work or in the many disciplines that depend on mathematics as a tool.

Quite apart from the limitations imposed on classroom practice by excessive reliance on textbooks, the very importance of the text as the primary medium of instruction poses unique challenges and opportunities:

- How can major school textbook series or course texts adapt quickly to changes in curricular goals or emerging technology?
- Are we on the verge of a post-Gutenberg revolution in which computer communications can deliver flexible interactive texts more readily and efficiently than the printing press?
- How can texts and software act as incentives rather than as brakes for the newly emerging standards for school mathematics?

Even while educators work to reduce the dominance of text-based learning in mathematics classrooms, publishers and teachers need to explore new modes of publication that will enable good innovative ideas to enter expeditiously into typical classroom practice. Texts, software, computer networks, and databases will blend in coming years into a new hybrid educational and information resource. It is already true that the most common application of school mathematics is to program formulas into computer spreadsheets. As texts evolve and software matures, both must be synchronized with forward-looking curricular and classroom objectives of mathematics education.

Assessment

Governors and political leaders in all fifty states are advocating assessment in order to raise expectations and evaluate programs. Tests serve many important purposes. They allow students to recognize personal success; they enable teachers to judge students' progress; they provide administrators means to measure the effectiveness of instruction; and they afford the public accountability for the use of public funds. When designed and used properly, tests and other assessment instruments provide feedback that is essential for any system to maintain steady progress toward its objectives.

"According to virtually all studies of the matter, textbooks have become the de facto curriculum of the public schools .... It is therefore critical that textbooks stimulate rather than deaden students' curiosity, and that teacher manuals encourage rather than squelch teachers' initiative and flexibility."

—*Harriet Tyson-Bernstein*

Teaching

Unfortunately, tests in mathematics education are rarely used in a manner appropriate to their design. Tests designed for diagnostic purposes are often used for evaluating programs; scores from self-selected populations (for example, takers of Scholastic Aptitude Tests) are used to compare districts and states; and commonly used achievement tests stress simple skills rather than sophisticated tasks, not because such skills are more important, but because they are easier to measure.

Tests are dear to the public; they produce winners and losers, as do sports playoffs, primary elections, and lotteries. Tests also symbolize commitment to things we value—to facts and information that we once learned and that we believe all children should still learn. In America (but not in other countries), objective, multiple-choice tests are the norm; they are efficient, economical, and seemingly fair.

Mathematical assessment in America relies excessively on misleading multiple-choice tests.

Nonetheless, multiple-choice tests as used in America lead to widespread abuses, which the public rarely recognizes:

- Tests become ends in themselves, not means to assess educational objectives. Knowing this, teachers often teach to the tests, not to the curriculum or to the children.
- Tests stress lower- rather than higher-order thinking, emphasizing student responses to test items rather than original thinking and expression.
- Test scores are sensitive to special coaching, which aggravates existing inequities in opportunities to learn.
- Tests reinforce in students, teachers, and the public the narrow image of mathematics as a subject with unique correct answers.
- Timed tests stressing speed inhibit learning for many students.

- Normed tests ignore the vast differences in rates at which children learn.
- Tests provide snapshots of performance under the most stressful environment for students rather than continuous information about performance in a supportive atmosphere.
- Poor test scores lead students to poor self-images, destroying rather than building confidence.

Similar problems arise when detailed learner outcomes rather than teacher judgments define the objectives of courses. Like items on objective tests, specific learner outcomes bias teacher effort and constrain student learning. The most important goals for mathematical learning cannot be atomized into tiny morsels of knowledge.

Too often, good intentions in testing can lead to very bad results. Minimal competency testing often leads to minimal performance, where the floor becomes a ceiling. In stressing the importance of basic skills, such tests fail to encourage able students to progress as far as they can. As political pressure for state assessment begins to encompass higher education, where assessment is even more complex, it is vitally important that the mathematical community agree on proper standards for assessment.

What is tested is what gets taught. Tests must measure what is most important.

. . . .

Assessment should be an integral part of teaching. It is the mechanism whereby teachers can learn *how* students think about mathematics as well as *what* students are able to accomplish. But tests also are used to compare classes and schools, to evaluate teachers, and to place students in future courses or careers. Because assessment is so pervasive and has such powerful impact on the lives of both students and teachers, it is very important that assessment practice align properly both with the purpose of the test and with curricular objectives.

Myth: Only objective tests yield reliable results.

Reality: Experience in evaluating student writing shows that trained readers judging whole essays produce results more aligned to the goal of high-quality writing than do objective exams of grammar and vocabulary. Similar experiences show that one can reliably judge scientific understanding by observing student teams in a laboratory. Effective means of assessing operational knowledge of mathematics must be similarly broad, reflecting the full environment in which employees and citizens will need to use their mathematical power.

Teaching

To assess development of a student's mathematical power, a teacher needs to use a mixture of means: essays, homework, projects, short answers, quizzes, blackboard work, journals, oral interviews, and group projects. Only broad-based assessment can reflect fairly the important, higher-order objectives of mathematics curricula.

As we need standards for curricula, so we need standards for assessment. We must ensure that tests measure what is of value, not just what is easy to test. If we want students to investigate, explore, and discover, assessment must not measure just mimicry mathematics. By confusing means and ends, by making testing more important than learning, present practice holds today's students hostage to yesterday's mistakes.

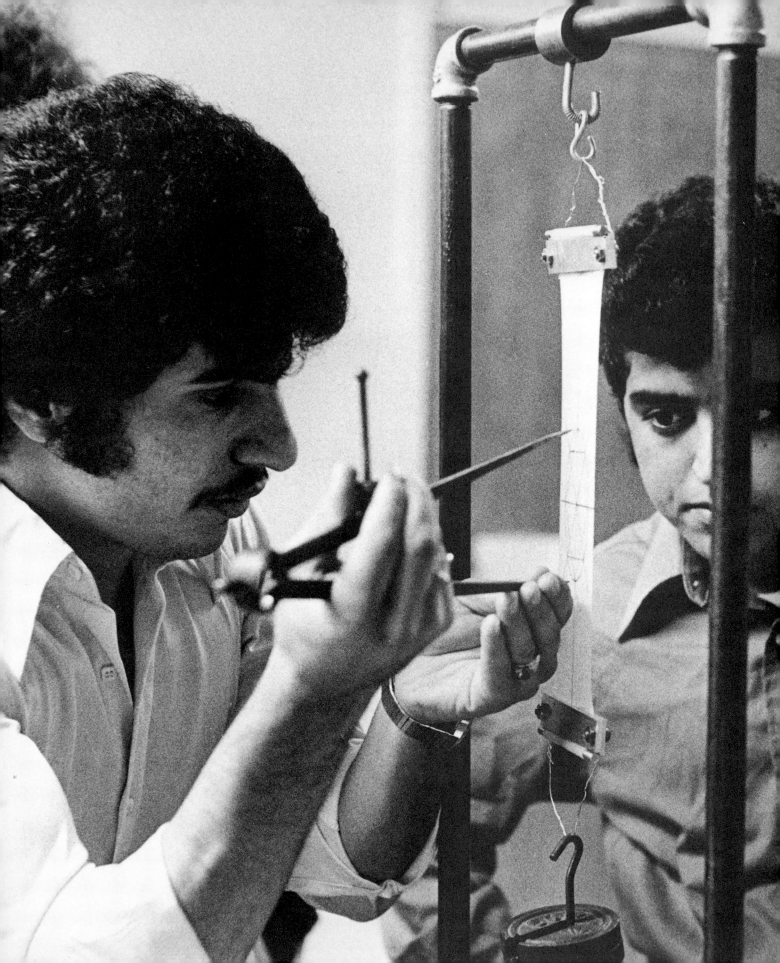

CHANGE

...mobilizing for curricular reform

Since the publication in 1983 of *A Nation at Risk,* Americans have known that fundamental changes must occur throughout all parts of our educational system in order to:

- Raise performance levels significantly in our nation's schools and colleges;
- Prepare young people for lifelong learning;
- Educate *all* students well, not only those identified as college bound;
- Create learning environments better suited to the needs of disadvantaged groups.

The future of our country depends strongly on our ability to bring about these fundamental changes in mathematics education.

C ontinual change is a natural and essential characteristic of mathematics education.

Because mathematics is one of the pillars of education, reform of education must include significant change in the way mathematics is taught and learned. As mathematics and society change continuously, so must mathematics education. Change is a natural state for education, not just a transition between old and new. To ensure continuous responsiveness in the future, mathematics education must adopt structures that will make change permanent; mathematics education must always respond to changes in science, in society, and in mathematics itself.

Challenges

Mathematics education in the United States is facing major challenges on nearly every front:

- Far too many students, disproportionately minority, leave school without having acquired the mathematical power necessary for productive lives.

> *"If an unfriendly foreign power had attempted to impose on America the mediocre educational performance that exists today, we might well have viewed it as an act of war. As it stands, we have allowed this to happen to ourselves."*
>
> —*A Nation at Risk*

Change

- The shortage of qualified mathematics teachers in the United States is serious—more serious than in any other area of education—and affects all levels from elementary school to graduate school.
- At a time when the percentage of minority students is increasing, the shortage of new minority teachers of mathematics is particularly acute.
- On average, U.S. students do not master mathematical fundamentals at a level sufficient to sustain our present technologically based society.
- When compared with other nations, U.S. students lag far behind in level of mathematical accomplishment; the resulting educational deficit reduces our ability to compete in international arenas.
- Public attitudes, which are reflected and magnified by the entertainment industry, encourage low expectations in mathematics. Only in mathematics is poor school performance socially acceptable.
- Curricula and instruction in our schools and colleges are years behind the times. They reflect neither the increased demand for higher-order thinking skills, nor the greatly expanded uses of the mathematical sciences, nor what we know about the best ways for students to learn mathematics.
- Calculators and computers have had virtually no impact on mathematics instruction in spite of their great potential to enrich, enlighten, and expand students' learning of mathematics.
- Common methods of evaluation—especially standardized, paper-and-pencil, multiple-choice tests of "basic skills"—are themselves obstacles to the teaching of higher-order thinking skills as well as to the use of calculators and computers.
- Undergraduate mathematics is intellectually stagnant, overgrown with stale courses that fail to stimulate the mathematical interests of today's students.

The information age is a mathematical age. Even as tomorrow's scientist and engineer will need extensive mathematics education, tomorrow's citizen will need a very different type of mathematical education to deal with mathematics-based tools, equipment, and techniques which will permeate the workplace. Far more than most citizens currently appreciate, mathematics education will play a substantial role in determining which doors are open and which are closed as students leave school and enter the world of work.

Counterproductive Beliefs

It is mistakenly thought, even by otherwise well-informed adults, that the mathematics they learned in school is adequate for their children. Parental and legislative pressures in the past few years, driven largely by frustration over declining test scores, have led to many rash actions:

- Increased numbers of required courses—where there is no agreement on what the added courses should contain or where capable teachers are to be found to teach them;
- Increased use of standardized tests—where there is very little understanding of what the tests contain or what they are capable of testing;
- Increased use of test scores, especially for teacher and school accountability—where there is little recognition that the tests reflect only a small part of curricular objectives.

The nation is in the grip of a testing mystique that has led to widespread misuse of standardized tests. Public pressures for "back-to-basics" stem from a very limited understanding of the challenges we face. Carried to the extreme, these pressures will rob our children of the opportunity to learn what they will need to know of mathematics in their adult lives.

Too often, what results from such actions are watered-down curricula, unreliable tests, and diminished morale. The only effective way in which these relatively ill-informed policies can be combated is through a systematic effort to develop in the public a deeper understanding of what works and what does not.

It will not be easy to develop better understanding. Often, public discussion about mathematics education masks

Myth: Increased requirements yield better prepared students.

Reality: Motivation almost always works better than requirements. Often, increased requirements have an effect quite the opposite of what was intended. In Wisconsin, for example, when the university increased from two to three years the number of courses required for admission and also increased the minimum grade point requirement, in some schools the number of students who elected four years of high school mathematics dropped. Once the three-year requirement was met, students skipped senior mathematics to protect their grade point averages. In Florida, increased requirements for graduation from high school have caused an increase in the number who drop out.

Change

Cultural Context

Competition and individualism, ingrained parts of traditional American culture, are reflected in typical mathematical courses where students work alone to solve set problems. Other cultures, including many which are now a growing part of the American scene, stress teamwork and group problem-solving. To the extent that mathematics instruction in the United States continues to stress individualism and competition over cooperation and teamwork, to that extent we continue to introduce unnecessary counterproductive practices for many in our multicultural nation.

Adult Attitudes

Too many Americans seem to believe that it does not really matter whether or not one learns mathematics. Only in America do adults openly proclaim their ignorance of mathematics ("I never was very good at math") as if it were some sort of merit badge. Parents and students in other countries know that mathematics matters.

a hidden agenda of values that have traditionally been carried forward by the school study of mathematics. Since the demise of Latin as a required school subject, it is to mathematics that many look as a vehicle to teach such qualities as precision, discipline, neatness, and accuracy. Mathematical truth—in popular caricature—is certain, absolute, unchanging, eternal. Mathematics appears to many to be a safe harbor of calm in a turbulent sea of social and educational change.

Proposals to change mathematics education appear to threaten time-honored values that are deeply embedded in the public image of mathematics. The need for change in mathematics education is too great to allow stereotypes of mathematics to impede reform.

It is important that the public learn not only about the need for change, but also about how the essential qualities of mathematics are conveyed by contemporary as well as traditional views of the field. As an active partner on the rapidly advancing frontier of science, mathematics is constantly expanding and changing. Mathematics education, in contrast, has been constrained by societal forces to such a degree that it has hardly changed at all. This contrast in the pace of change virtually ensures that mathematics education is perpetually out of date.

N..
aive policies rooted in myth impede reform of mathematics education.
....

As a subject with an extensive and substantial history, mathematics more than any other science has been taught as an ancient discipline. A nation that persists in this view of mathematics is destined to fall behind scientifically and economically. Parents who persist in this view deny their children the opportunity to develop and prosper in the information age.

The American Way

The development of more effective strategies for revitalizing mathematics education must be based in part on an understanding of why it is so difficult in the United States to bring about change in education. The truth we shrink from confronting is that most previous reform efforts have failed. A properly skeptical public will rightly ask why any new effort is more likely to succeed. Part of the difficulty we face in mathematics education is a natural reflection of our constitutional dilemma: to reconcile local authority with national need.

Most other countries have either national curricula or nationwide curricular guidelines. Curricular development is typically a routine function of a ministry of education which taps the best brainpower in the nation to develop complete sets of texts and other resource materials for classroom use. Specific day-to-day syllabi and teacher guides are often provided to schools; in some cases, these syllabi are actually mandated by a ministry of education. In many countries, all children in the same grade study essentially the same material in almost the same way. Such practice, common around the world, reveals a strong tradition of a "top-down" approach in education.

In the United States, with our traditional and legal decentralization of education, we go about things very differently. Every summer, thousands of teachers work in small teams for periods ranging from one week to two months, charged by their school districts to write new mathematics curricula. These teacher teams usually have little training in the complicated process of curricular development, little or no help in coping with changing needs, and little to fall back on except existing textbooks, familiar programs, and tradition. The consequence usually is the unquestioned acceptance of what already exists as the main body of the new curriculum, together with a little tinkering around the edges. Many school districts simply adopt series of textbooks as *the* curriculum, making no effort to engage the staff in rethinking curricula; in those places, the *status quo* certainly reigns.

International Expectations

Average students in other countries often learn as much mathematics as the best students learn in the United States. Data from the Second International Mathematics Study (1982) show that the performance of the top 5 percent of U.S. students is matched by the top 50 percent of students in Japan. Our very best students—the top 1 percent—scored lowest of the top 1 percent in all participating countries. All U.S. students—whether below, at, or above average—can and must learn more mathematics.

T. . . . .
raditional U.S. approaches to curricular
change make reform impossible.

. . . .

The American process of curricular reform might be described as a weak form of a grass-roots approach. The record shows that this system does not work. It is not our teachers who are at fault. In fact, teachers *should* play a dominant role in curricular decision-making. But teachers who work in summer curricular projects are being given an unrealistic task in an impossible time frame, with only the familiar *status quo* to guide them.

In static times, in periods of unchanging demands, perhaps our grass-roots efforts would suffice to keep the curriculum current. In today's climate, in which technology and research are causing unprecedented change in the central methods and applications of mathematics, present U.S. practice is totally inadequate. International comparisons of student performance in mathematics—for example, the Second International Mathematics Study—show that U.S. students lag far behind their counterparts in other industrialized countries. The top-down systems have beaten us hands down.

Modern Mathematics

Curricular reforms undertaken in the two decades from 1955 to 1975 under the slogans of "modern mathematics" or "new math" left a mixed legacy to American mathematics education. The movement sprang from many roots and took on many different (and sometimes opposing) forms. Implementation was quite uneven, as were results.

Looking back, one can identify several important areas of success and failure:

- Certain important seeds sowed during this period (for example, renewed emphasis on geometry, probability, and statistics) have taken root and are now on the verge of blossoming.

"Most students seem to think that mathematics courses are chiefly designed to winnow out the weak and grind down the ungifted. We need a change in attitude."

—*Edward E. David, Jr.*

- Too often, the proposed means to achieve deeper understanding (for example, sets and commutative law) became ends in themselves, thus opening mathematics education to public ridicule.
- Innovative applications of mathematics to nontraditional fields (for example, to biology and business) became accepted as part of the content of school mathematics.
- By moving some parts of school curricula into unfamiliar areas, mathematics educators lost the confidence of their most important ally—parents.

Both educators and parents can learn from the experiences of the modern mathematics era, but the lessons are not so simple as conventional wisdom often suggests.

Lessons from the Past

The history of the past twenty-five years of curricular reform gives us only negative examples from which to learn. Few traces remain of the expensive major curricular development projects so prominent in the 1960's and 1970's. These projects tried to develop, on a national scale, complete curricula (including instructional materials) that could be adopted by school districts. But the theorists and planners who developed these curricula were naive about the process of change; big curricular projects failed to take root in American schools because they were transplanted fully grown into an environment better suited to locally grown methods.

Where teachers were not directly a part of the development procedure, where their ownership of the product was not ensured, where teachers considered district acceptance of the curriculum as a top-down imposition, the revised programs did not last. Where parents could not (or did not) understand the need for change or the reasons new curricular emphases were chosen, resentment and anger resulted and a solid conviction set in that if the "old math" was good enough for parents, it was good enough for their children.

As the United States enters a new period of change in mathematics education, we can benefit from several lessons drawn from these previous attempts. First, free-standing, full-service curricular development projects adopted intact by school districts do not work. Second, a superficial, district-by-district approach to curricular overhaul is potentially disastrous, given the demanding nature of what educators face.

E ffective reform requires strong leadership by teachers, parents, professionals, and politicians.

Third, any successful effort to improve mathematics curricula and instruction in the schools will require an extensive public information campaign that reaches all the varied constituencies of mathematics education. These diverse publics must be convinced in understandable language that a very different mathematics education is both better and necessary for their children and for the country. Effective change requires a great deal from the public:

- Conviction of the need for change;
- Consensus on high-quality mathematics education for everyone;
- Skepticism of "quick fixes" and simplistic solutions;
- Awareness of the general nature of needed changes;
- Support for investment of necessary resources;
- Recognition of the need for continuing leadership at the national level.

General reaction to the many recent calls for school reform has been uneven and fragmented. The pattern of unfocused reaction shows that it is not enough just to get the public's attention. Public concern is a necessary, but by no means sufficient, condition for meaningful educational change. Too often, a partially informed public becomes a poorly informed electorate. The time is ripe for a new approach to curricular reform, one that establishes appropriate national expectations supported by broad public support among parents, teachers, and taxpayers.

Transitions

In order to meet the challenges of our time, mathematics education is already beginning to negotiate several difficult transitions which will dominate the process of change during the remainder of this century. Only gradually, by extensive experience, will teachers find the most effective point along each transition path. Although no one can say in advance where the best balance lies, it is quite clear that present practice is at an ineffective extreme.

Transition 1: *The focus of school mathematics is shifting from a dualistic mission—minimal mathematics for the majority, advanced mathematics for a few—to a singular focus on a significant common core of mathematics for all students.*

The needs of industry for a quantitatively literate work force compel schools to provide more mathematical education to more students than ever before. Accomplishing this will pose significant challenges to:

- Develop a core of mathematics appropriate for all students throughout each year of school;
- Educate well a significantly larger fraction of the population;
- Stimulate able students with the excitement and challenge of mathematics;
- Differentiate instruction by approach and speed, not by curricular goals;
- Select topics and approaches of broad interest and effectiveness.

Transition 2: *The teaching of mathematics is shifting from an authoritarian model based on "transmission of knowledge" to a student-centered practice featuring "stimulation of learning."*

In both schools and colleges, classrooms of passive students who are expected to sit and absorb rules which appear as arbitrary dicta from on high are gradually giving way to learning environments that:

- Encourage students to explore;
- Help students verbalize their mathematical ideas;

Voice of Experience

"Math Achievement through Problem Solving is an activity-oriented process that uses small groups to focus on nonroutine problems. It was designed for students with bad work habits who seem to get very little out of traditional high school algebra. We've found out that a lot of these students know much more than we thought, and many know less. We've been surprised at the high level of thinking that goes on in some of these students."
—Jon Brice

- Show students that many mathematical questions have more than one right answer;
- Provide evidence that mathematics is alive and exciting;
- Teach students through experience the importance of careful reasoning and disciplined understanding;
- Build confidence in *all* students that they *can* learn mathematics.

Transition 3: *Public attitudes about mathematics are shifting from indifference and hostility to recognition of the important role that mathematics plays in today's society.*

Although the burden of unfavorable school experiences continues to color public opinion about mathematics, contemporary events are sending different messages which are gradually being heard:

- In other nations where more is expected, more mathematics is learned;
- As the role of science and technology expands, so does the importance of mathematics;
- To function as an informed citizen, numeracy is as important as literacy.

As attitudes about the importance of mathematics improve, so will expectations for mathematics education.

Transition 4: *The teaching of mathematics is shifting from preoccupation with inculcating routine skills to developing broad-based mathematical power.*

Mathematical power requires that students be able to discern relations, reason logically, and use a broad spectrum of mathematical methods to solve a wide variety of non-routine problems. The repertoire of skills which now undergird mathematical power includes not only some traditional paper-and-pencil skills, but also many broader and more powerful capabilities. Today's students must be able to:

- Perform mental calculations and estimates with proficiency;
- Decide when an exact answer is needed and when an estimate is more appropriate;

- Know which mathematical operations are appropriate in particular contexts;
- Use a calculator correctly, confidently, and appropriately;
- Estimate orders of magnitude to confirm mental or calculator results;
- Use tables, graphs, spreadsheets, and statistical techniques to organize, interpret, and present numerical information;
- Judge the validity of quantitative results presented by others;
- Use computer software for mathematical tasks;
- Formulate specific questions from vague problems;
- Select effective problem-solving strategies.

Transition 5: *The teaching of mathematics is shifting from emphasis on tools for future courses to greater emphasis on topics that are relevant to students' present and future needs.*

Most mathematics should be presented in the context of its uses, with appreciation of mathematics as a deductive logical system built up slowly through the rising levels of education. Examples of areas deserving greater emphasis are:

- Probability, which facilitates reasoning about uncertainty and assessment of risk;
- Exploratory data analysis and statistics, which facilitate reasoning about data;
- Model-building, which facilitates systematic, structured understanding of complex situations;
- Operations research, which facilitates planning of complex tasks and achieving performance objectives;
- Discrete mathematics, which facilitates understanding of most applications of computers.

These new topics imply that observation and experimentation will be important in future mathematics programs and that school mathematics will draw closer to other school subjects, especially to science.

Transition 6: *The teaching of mathematics is shifting from primary emphasis on paper-and-pencil calculations to full use of calculators and computers.*

Mathematics teachers at all levels—from elementary school to university—are adapting their teaching methods

Voice of Experience

"I approach each problem as if I didn't already know the conventional solution. The students are much more involved and excited. They become creators. It's as described by Felix Klein: The mathematician himself does not work in a rigorous, deductive manner, but rather uses fantasy."
—Kenneth Cummins

Change

to include both new approaches to instruction as well as new subject matter appropriate to future-oriented curricula. Calculators and computers make new modes of instruction feasible at the same time that they inject into the learning environment a special sense of wonder which goes with healthy development of mathematical power.

Calculators and computers should be used in ways that anticipate continuing rapid change due to technological developments. Technology should be used not because it is seductive, but because it can enhance mathematical learning by extending each student's mathematical power. Calculators and computers are not substitutes for hard work or precise thinking, but challenging tools to be used for productive ends.

Transition 7: *The public perception of mathematics is shifting from that of a fixed body of arbitrary rules to a vigorous active science of patterns.*

Mathematics is a living subject which seeks to understand patterns that permeate both the world around us and the mind within us. Although the language of mathematics is based on rules that must be learned, it is important for motivation that students move beyond rules to be able to express things in the language of mathematics. This transformation suggests changes in both curricular content and instructional style. It involves renewed effort to focus on:

- Seeking solutions, not just memorizing procedures;
- Exploring patterns, not just learning formulas;
- Formulating conjectures, not just doing exercises.

As teaching begins to reflect these emphases, students will have opportunities to study mathematics as an exploratory, dynamic, evolving discipline rather than as a rigid, absolute, closed body of laws to be memorized. They will be encouraged to see mathematics as a science, not as a canon, and to recognize that mathematics is really about patterns and not merely about numbers.

ACTION  *...moving into the 21st century*

Over the next two decades, the nation's schools, colleges, and universities will undergo major transitions in their mathematics programs—transitions that will involve fundamental changes in curricular content, in modes of instruction, in teacher education, in professional development, in methods of assessment, and in public attitudes. Not only will calculators and computers displace some of the computational drill that currently dominates the curriculum, but also their presence will stimulate new approaches to understanding mathematics and to solving problems. The dramatic advances that have been made in the mathematical sciences over the past forty years will start to be felt in the schools, in the form of new and exciting ways to help young minds perceive and order the universe around them.

If such transitions are to become reality, all major components of mathematics education—curricula, teaching, teacher education, testing, textbooks, and software—must change significantly in some reasonably coordinated manner. National leadership is needed to coordinate efforts by the primary agents for change and to garner support for them by government, business, industry, and the public.

I.......................................
n the next decade, the United States has a historic opportunity to revitalize mathematics education.

....

Although many parts of education need improvement, there are at this time both a particular urgency and a special opportunity for reform of mathematics education. Since mathematics is the foundation of science and technology, reform is needed to prepare the more highly skilled work force that the nation now needs. Because of emerging general agreement within the mathematics, mathematics education, and related professional communities on goals for mathematics education and means for achieving them, there is at this time a special opportunity for the nation to push ahead boldly in this area of education.

National Goals

Our national goal must be to make U.S. mathematics education the best in the world. Nothing less will be adequate to fulfill American aspirations. To achieve this goal will require significant actions that respond to a three-tiered challenge to:

- Make mathematics education effective for all Americans;
- Improve significantly students' mathematical achievement;
- Develop new curricula appropriate to the mathematical needs of the twenty-first century.

> O·····························
> ur national goal must be to make U.S. mathematics education the best in the world.
> ·····························

American education is a loosely coupled system grounded in state and local autonomy, although important factors (textbooks, standardized testing, teacher education, and university admissions requirements) have nationwide influence. To change mathematics education in the United States, one must influence not only teachers, but also a host of other special interest groups that control parts of the educational system: state and local agencies, teachers and administrators, local and state school boards, colleges and universities, textbook publishers, software developers, professional societies, test-makers, state legislators, employers, parents, and the general public.

Actions designed to begin these transitions must be based on a broad understanding of the total American system of mathematics education. Unless change is based on a systematic overview of all pertinent issues and an assessment of current programs, it will have very little chance of achieving national impact.

Reaching Consensus

High-quality mathematics education requires national consensus on objectives and standards, leaving wide latitude for local variation in means of implementation. Without common standards, different communities will move in different directions, inevitably widening the gap in mathematical power available to children raised and educated in different circumstances. National consensus on common objectives should make possible policies that will ensure that all students benefit equally from the opportunities provided by mathematics.

Building national consensus is the first step in renewal of school mathematics.

Although pressure for change is high, little consensus exists on what mathematics students ought to learn now, much less on what they will need for the future. Lack of national focus has created such disparities among standards that it is difficult to discuss curricula in meaningful and productive contexts. Teachers have received such mixed signals that even the best of them often do not know which choices to make in those few classes where they have some discretion over what to teach.

The new *Curriculum and Evaluation Standards for School Mathematics,* being published in early 1989 by the National Council of Teachers of Mathematics (NCTM), focuses national attention on specific objectives for school mathematics. That report, the draft of which has been reviewed extensively by teachers and the public, has received widespread support in the mathematical and educational communities. It represents the first effort ever to establish national expectations for school mathematics.

In keeping with American school traditions, the *Standards* report is not the result of government edict, but the product

Action

of the nation's mathematics teachers themselves. It leaves much leeway for local initiative in implementation and for teacher ownership of specific curricula. Through the *Standards*, parents and teachers will be able to understand in concrete terms what a school mathematics program might look like if it is to serve our national objectives adequately. The ensuing public discussion on feasibility, appropriateness, costs, and benefits will provide an unprecedented opportunity to forge national consensus on goals and objectives for school mathematics.

National Strategy

New strategies for renewal of mathematics education must be based on what we have learned about making changes in the extremely decentralized U.S. system where local and state agencies control education. Two special strengths of American mathematics education should underpin any movement for renewal:

- The creative efforts of many teachers, schools, and projects around the country.
- The strength of coordinated national leadership which has evolved within the communities of mathematicians and mathematics educators.

Together, these resources provide an "augmented grassroots" model of curricular development, harnessing the power of a centralized system with the flexibility and initiative of the decentralized U.S. tradition.

The objective of our national strategy must be to make significant improvements in mathematics education on a national scale. To do this, we must first reach consensus on the transitions required to revitalize mathematics education and then help local educational leaders move mathematics education through these transitions. Inevitably, this process will lead the American public into uncharted territory, paving a new road for mathematics education that balances national goals with local jurisdiction.

Why Not Just Imitate Japan?

International studies of mathematics and science education show that, when compared with students in other countries, U.S. students do very poorly while Japanese students do very well. One natural response, therefore, is to think that we could improve our educational system by imitating Japan.

These same studies, however, document that the social context of education has a greater influence on student performance than does actual classroom practice. Parental attitudes, student expectations, and teacher self-respect are among the most significant factors in quality education and they depend uniquely on culture.

Imitating others is no solution. The United States must find a strategy that builds on the traditions of this country, one whose strength lies in this nation's unique tradition of local initiative and decentralized authority.

90

Reform of mathematics education requires voluntary local implementation of common national standards.

The key to success is voluntary acceptance of a common framework to guide local choices:

- *National Standards.* School mathematics programs across the nation should share a common philosophy and framework, a universal set of interrelated concepts and methods, held together by a simple workable philosophy, yet flexible enough to allow for local and regional variations. In a highly mobile society, the basic framework should be transportable and adaptable.

- *Local Implementation.* Changes in mathematics curricula must be proposed and undertaken freely by those who bear direct responsibility for curricula in the schools. A deep sense of identification with those changes must be developed within the entire community. In particular, teachers and parents need to be involved in adaptation and decision-making in a thorough and comprehensive way.

Implementation will require more than good will and community dialogue; it will need professional leadership of teachers operating in a transformed school environment. No one should underestimate the complexity of the challenge; effective reform will be truly difficult to accomplish. Few teachers in today's schools have the authority or resources necessary to carry out this agenda. But as schools evolve from a model with teachers as hired hands to one in which teachers function as professional educators, schools should welcome the challenge to implement national standards for mathematics education.

Support Structures

In order for this strategy to work, the United States must develop new national support structures to help states and localities promote excellence in mathematics education for all students. These structures must assure appropriate consistency among the nation's many different school districts, yet encourage a sense of local ownership by allowing adaptation to local preferences.

Important parts of this national structure are in place already, while other parts will emerge in coming months and years. Professional organizations (the National Council of Teachers of Mathematics, the American Mathematical Society, the Mathematical Association of America, the Society of Industrial and Applied Mathematics, the American Statistical Association, the Conference Board of the Mathematical Sciences) are actively engaged in projects that seek to improve the teaching of mathematics. Related actions of other groups such as the National Congress of Parents and Teachers, the National Governors' Association, the National School Boards Association, and the American Association for the Advancement of Science will ensure a vigorous national dialogue, which is a necessary prerequisite to national consensus.

As schools are not the sole source of America's problems in mathematics education, neither can they be the sole vehicle for renewal. Informal, nonschool-based undertakings that support school-based mathematics education can be found in clubs, churches, and scouting. Community organizations effectively complement schools, reaching youth—especially minorities—who find school uninspiring. Being outside the formal public structures, community organizations offer a testing ground to validate the power of innovative or unconventional ideas.

Building national consensus requires effective national leadership.

To stimulate informed debate about curricular change, the Mathematical Sciences Education Board is preparing two reports on concepts and principles of mathematics suitable for the education of students who will work in the twenty-first century. One, a statement of philosophy and curricular frameworks, provides a general structure that can guide curriculum development for the future. The other, on major strands of mathematical thought, is intended to stimulate creative development of new curricula that embody a broader interpretation of mathematics. These strands—chance, change, shape, quantity, dimension—are examples of deep ideas of mathematics that could become organizing principles for some future mathematics curriculum.

These actions of many different groups—representing mathematicians, scientists, educators, and administrators—will form the basis of a national consensus for new directions in mathematics education.

Leadership

Real change requires action by everyone involved in mathematics education. Current efforts to forge national consensus will not in themselves transform what happens in schools or colleges. Change in the institutions of education must come about as the result of intensive debate within each institution. There is plenty of work for everyone:

STUDENTS:
Study mathematics every school year.
Discover the mathematics that is all around us.
Use mathematics in other classes and in daily life.
Study a broad variety of mathematical subjects.

TEACHERS:
Talk with each other about mathematics.
Examine current practice and debate new proposals.
Engage students actively in the process of learning.

PARENTS:
Demand that schools meet the new *NCTM Standards*.
Encourage children to continue studying mathematics.
Support teachers who seek curricular improvements.
Expect homework to be more than routine computation.

PRINCIPALS:
Provide opportunities for teachers to work together.
Become educated on issues in mathematics education.
Support innovation.
Encourage paired teaching in elementary school.

SUPERINTENDENTS:
Stimulate public discussion of mathematics education.
Provide resources for curricular innovation.
Support a climate of change.

SCHOOL BOARDS:
Establish appropriate standards for mathematics.
Align assessment with curricular goals.
Support innovation and professional development.

COMMUNITY ORGANIZATIONS:
Enrich mathematical opportunities for all students.
Support local efforts to improve mathematics education.
Explain to the public the need for change.

STATE SCHOOL OFFICERS:
Promote adoption of *NCTM's Standards*.
Encourage use of elementary mathematics specialists.
Speak out publicly about mathematics education.
Stress assessment of higher-order thinking.

COLLEGE AND UNIVERSITY FACULTY:
Make introductory courses attractive and effective.
Restore integrity to the undergraduate program.
Lecture less; try other teaching methods.
Link scholarship to teaching.

COLLEGE AND UNIVERSITY ADMINISTRATORS:
Reward curricular innovation and good teaching.
Recognize that mathematics classes need computer labs.
Diminish reliance on underprepared, part-time faculty.
Emphasize and improve teacher education.

BUSINESS AND INDUSTRY:
Encourage students to study mathematics and science.
Do not steal good teachers by hiring them away.
Support local efforts to secure funds for education.
Support strong continuing education, not remediation.
Provide internship opportunities for teachers.

STATE LEGISLATORS:
Work with school leaders to support effective programs.
Recognize that mathematics education is an investment.
Resist pressures for simplistic cures.

GOVERNORS:
Provide resources to encourage change.
Demand new standards for mathematics education.
Lead the public to make wise choices among priorities.
Create enrichment programs for able students.

CONGRESS:
Stress education as an essential investment.
Support mathematics education at all levels.
Reward effective programs.

THE PRESIDENT:
Meet with state governors to affirm the national agenda.
Focus public attention on mathematics education.
Stress education as crucial to national security.

Taking Action

Once vigorous dialogue and grass-roots actions begin forging national consensus on goals for school mathematics, several important national objectives must be addressed:

- Establish new standards for school mathematics.
- Upgrade the teaching profession.
- Make assessment responsive to future needs.
- Strengthen collegiate mathematics.

The first of these will emerge, with sufficient effort, following public dialogue about the NCTM *Standards.* The second is currently being advocated through the work of the National Board for Professional Teaching Standards. The third, assessment, may require a new, cooperative, national mechanism to unlock the stranglehold that state and national testing programs—largely secret—have on today's classrooms. Finally, strengthening college and university mathematics—including specific attention to those who become teachers, how they teach, and what they teach—is the primary task of the National Research Council's Committee on the Mathematical Sciences in the Year 2000 (MS 2000).

Action

"*Children are the future. Everything we do is for them and everything that will be done will be done by them.*"

—*Clay Morgan*

Efforts to change must proceed steadily for many years, on many levels simultaneously, with broad involvement of all constituencies at each stage. First comes serious discussion; then, compromise and consensus; finally, action and change. Even as different groups work to improve curricular standards, the teaching profession, assessment practices, and collegiate mathematics, other groups must help focus the diverse efforts of business, industry, government, volunteer organizations, and educational organizations on common objectives. As there is no royal road to geometry, so there are no quick fixes for mathematics education.

Both for reasons of international competitiveness and scientific leadership, the United States must move quickly to improve the state of mathematics education. It takes a generation to complete the mathematical education of a single individual. The first high school graduates of the next century entered elementary school in 1988. No longer can we afford to sit idly by while our children move through school without receiving mathematical preparation appropriate for the twenty-first century.

The challenges are clear. The choices are before us. It is time to act.

REFERENCES

REFERENCES

...documenting the challenge

A report of this nature touches on issues related to a very broad literature, from demographic analyses to mathematical research, from educational policy to pedagogical theories. Because of heightened interest in educational reform and rapid changes in the mathematical sciences, this literature has expanded greatly in recent years. While many of the issues addressed in the report have been studied and thought about for a very long time, some of the most urgent matters (for example, changing demographics and the impact of computing) have emerged only in recent years.

Virtually every issue treated in *Everybody Counts* has roots in studies or reports of the past ten years. Some matters come directly from this literature; many other statements, however, are more the product of expert consensus than of documentable research. As a result, the references to this report provide not so much a record of evidence as a resource for action.

To guide readers to the most current sources, the bibliography stresses works published in the 1980's. The absence of much of the older literature is a result of this choice, not a judgment about relative merits of classics in the field. Pointers to important earlier analyses can readily be found among the books and papers in the bibliography.

Notes

The following notes suggest references that relate to particular sections. Because of the complex interactions among sections of this report—interactions which are reflected also in many of the references—the linkage of references to report sections is at most a very rough guide.

OPPORTUNITY

Context for Change: Nat. Comm. (1983); NSB (1983).
Mathematics for Tomorrow: Koerner (1981); Steen (1988).
A Pump, Not a Filter: Mosaic (1987); OTA (1988); Turner (1986).
Numeracy: Bennett (1984); Bennett (1987); Boyer (1983); Boyer (1987); Cockcroft (1986); Heckert (1984); IEA (1988); Miller (1988).
Attitudes: McKnight (1987).

References

Goals: Johnston (1987); Resnick (1987); Romberg (1988).
Students at Risk: ACE (1988); Norman (1988); Oaxaca (1988).

HUMAN RESOURCES

Demographic Trends: Coyle (1986); Galambos (1980); Hodgkinson (1985); Hum. Cap. (1988); Johnston (1987); Jones (1982); Taylor (1984).
Minorities: Baratz (1986); Ford (1986); Ford (1987); Kozlov (1987); Malcom (1984); McBay (1986); NSF (1988); What Works (1987).
Women: Harnisch (1986); Oaxaca (1988); Widnall (1988).
Disabled Persons: Oaxaca (1988).
Graduate Students: Case (1988); Simon (1987); Stewart (1987).
Supply and Demand: Connors (1988).
Equity and Excellence: Oaxaca (1988); Widnall (1988).

MATHEMATICS

Our Invisible Culture: Bd. Math. Sci. (1986); Murnane (1988).
From Abstraction to Application: Bd. Math. Sci. (1986); Bd. Math. Sci. (1988); Browder (1983); Feigenbaum (1988); Gleick (1987); Peterson (1988); Rheinboldt (1984); Rheinboldt (1985); Steen (1988).
Computers: Heppenheimer (1985); Howson (1986); Zorn (1987).
The Mathematical Community: Albers (1987); David (1984); Gilfeather (1987); Madison (1989).
Undergraduate Mathematics: Albers (1985); Assoc. Amer. Coll. (1985); David (1988); Lucas (1980); NSB (1986); NSB (1987).

CURRICULUM

Philosophy: CBMS (1984); Cockcroft (1986); D'Ambrosio (1981); Davis (1988); Freudenthal (1973); Freudenthal (1983); Romberg (1983); Romberg (1984).
Standards: CBMS (1983); Chambers (1986); Crosswhite (1986); Denham (1985); Dossey (1988); Naumer (1986); NCTM (1989); Tyson-Bernstein (1988).
Elementary Education: Byrd (1987); Flanders (1987); Steen (1986).
Secondary Education: California (1982); CEEB (1985); Dessart (1983); Dossey (1988); Hirsch (1985); Howson (1986); Maurer (1983); SUNY (1983).
Higher Education: Albers (1985); Assoc. Amer. Coll. (1985); CUPM (1981); Davis-Van Atta (1985); Howson (1988); May (1961); NIE (1984); Ralston (1983); Steen (1988).

TEACHING

Understanding Mathematics: Fey (1981); ICMI (1979).

Learning Mathematics: MSEB (1987); Schoenfeld (1987); Tobias (1988); What Works (1986).

Engaging Students: Burton (1984); Cooney (1988); Davis (1984); Ginsburg (1983); Grouws (1988); Kilpatrick (1987); Lampert (1986); Lesh (1983); Mason (1982); Mestre (1987); Nisbett (1987); Resnick (1983); Resnick (1987); Schoenfeld (1985).

Impact of Computers: Fey (1984); Howson (1986); NCTM (1986); Smith (1988); Wilf (1982); Zorn (1987).

Education of Teachers: Carnegie (1986); Cooney (1985); CUPM (1983); Holmes (1986); Shulman (1986); Thompson (1984).

Resources: Tyson-Bernstein (1988).

Assessment: Charles (1988); James (1987); Murnane (1988); Romberg (1987); State Educ. Assess. Ctr. (1987).

CHANGE

Challenges: AAAS (1984); Kelly (1986); NCTM (1981); NSB (1982); NSB (1983); NSF (1979).

Counterproductive Beliefs: Stevenson (1986); Willoughby (1981).

The American Way: GAO (1984); Wirszup (1987).

Modern Mathematics: NACOME (1975).

Lessons from the Past: Crosswhite (1985); IEA (1988); NACOME (1975); Tammadge (1977).

Transitions: AAAS (1982); Ralston (1988); Romberg (1988).

ACTION

National Goals: NSB (1983); Steen (1987).

Reaching Consensus: AAAS (1987); ACS (1984); MAA (1978); NCTM (1980); NCTM (1989); Price (1981).

National Strategy: Kelly (1986); Knapp (1987).

Support Structures: CCSO (1987); Driscoll (1987); Nat. Gov. Assoc. (1987); Sanders (1987).

Leadership: What Works (1987).

Taking Action: Carnegie (1988); NCTM (1989).

References

Sources

To keep the text uncluttered, it contains few reference notes concerning individuals or data. For those who want further information, the following notes identify people, data, and figures mentioned explicitly in the text:

p. 1 Lester Thurow is an economist and dean of the Sloan School of Management at the Massachusetts Institute of Technology.

p. 2 The quotation from *Workforce 2000* is from p. 99 of Johnston (1987).

p. 6 Robert M. White is president of the National Academy of Engineering. The quotation is from keynote remarks he presented at the October 1987 National Research Council colloquium "Calculus for a New Century"; see p. 9 of Steen (1988).

p. 6 Data for the Mathematics Pipeline graph are derived from Thomas D. Snyder, *Digest of Education Statistics 1987,* Center for Education Statistics, May 1987, and from Alexander W. Astin, Kenneth C. Green, and William S. Korn, *The American Freshman: Twenty Year Trends,* American Council on Education, January 1987.

p. 7 The quotation from *Mathematics Counts* is from p. 11 of Cockcroft (1986).

p. 9 William R. Graham was science adviser to President Reagan. The quotation is from p. 247 of Graham (1987).

p. 11 Some of the "Back to School" sample problems were adapted from curriculum material under development by the University of Chicago School Mathematics Project.

p. 12 Jaime Escalante is a mathematics teacher at Garfield High School in East Los Angeles; his work was featured in the film *Stand and Deliver.* The quotation is from an interview in the July-August 1988 issue of *N.S.F. Directions.*

p. 13 The quotation from *One Third of a Nation* is from American Council on Education (1988).

p. 17 Data for the graph on Intended Mathematics Majors of Top High School Seniors are taken from *Science and Engineering Indicators—1987,* National Science Foundation, 1987.

p. 18 Data for the graph on Shifting Student Interests are taken from Alexander W. Astin, et al., *The American Freshman: National Norms for Fall 1987,* American Council on Education, December 1987.

p. 18 The quotation from *Workforce 2000* is from p. 95 of Johnston (1987).

p. 19 Harold L. Hodgkinson is senior fellow and director of the Center for Demographic Policy at the Institute for Educational Leadership. The quotation is from Hodgkinson (1985).

p. 20 Jaime Escalante; see p. 12.

p. 20 Philip Uri Treisman is associate director of the Professional Development Project at the University of California at Berkeley.

p. 21 Sheila Widnall is professor of aeronautical engineering at the Massachusetts Institute of Technology and past president of the American Association for the Advancement of Science. The quotation is from Widnall (1988).

p. 22 Data for the graph on Distribution of Ph.D. Degrees are taken from "1987 Annual AMS-MAA Survey—First Report," *Notices of the American Mathematical Society,* November 1987.

p. 23 I. Richard Savage is professor of statistics at Yale University and a member of the Conference Board of the Mathematical Sciences Advisory Committee on Disabled Mathematicians.

p. 25 Data for the graph on Decline in Mathematics Ph.D.'s are adapted from the series "Annual AMS-MAA Survey Reports" 1973-1986, *Notices of the American Mathematical Society.*

p. 27 Data for the graph on Bachelor's Degrees come from Thomas D. Snyder, *Digest of Education Statistics 1987,* May 1987.

p. 29 Harvey Keynes is professor of mathematics at the University of Minnesota and director of the UMTYMP, the University of Minnesota Talented Youth Mathematics Project.

p. 33 Nobel laureate Richard Feynman was professor of physics at the California Institute of Technology.

p. 35 The quotation by Eugene Wigner is on p. 14 of "The Unreasonable Effectiveness of Mathematics in the Natural Sciences," *Communications on Pure and Applied Mathematics,* 13 (1960).

p. 35 Stephen Hawking, a cosmologist, is Lucasian Professor of Mathematics at Cambridge University.

p. 39 The quotation from *Workforce 2000* is from p. 116 of Johnston (1987).

p. 40 Edward E. David, Jr., is president of EED, Inc. He was formerly president of Exxon Research and Engineering Company and was science adviser to President Nixon. The quotation is from p. 1122 of David (1988).

p. 44 See NCTM (1989).

p. 51 Data for the graph on Undergraduate Mathematics are adapted from Albers (1987), the 1985 annual survey of the Conference Board of the Mathematical Sciences.

p. 67 See Tyson-Bernstein (1988), pp. 11-12.

p. 70 Ray Whinnem is principal of Martin Elementary School and K-6 mathematics coordinator for Manchester Public Schools, Manchester, Connecticut.

p. 73 See National Commission (1983).

p. 74 John A. Dossey is professor of mathematics at Illinois State University and past president of the National Council of Teachers of Mathematics (1986–1988).

p. 77 For data on international comparisons, see McKnight (1987) and Crosswhite (1986).

p. 78 See David (1988), p. 1122; also, see note for p. 40.

p. 81 Jon Brice is a mathematics teacher at Marion High School, Marion, Indiana.

p. 83 Kenneth Cummins is emeritus professor of mathematical sciences at Kent State University.

p. 84 Marc S. Tucker is president of the National Center on Education and the Economy.

p. 96 Clay Morgan is a writer from McCall, Idaho. This quotation is adapted from remarks delivered at the September 29, 1988, launch of the shuttle Discovery.

References

Bibliography

Albers, Donald J.; Anderson, Richard D.; Loftsgaarden, Don O. *Undergraduate Programs in the Mathematical and Computer Sciences: The 1985-1986 Survey.* MAA Notes No. 7. Washington, D.C.: Mathematical Association of America, 1987.

Albers, Donald J.; Rodi, Stephen B.; Watkins, Ann E. (eds.). *New Directions in Two-Year College Mathematics.* New York: Springer-Verlag, 1985.

American Association for the Advancement of Science. *A Report on the Crisis in Mathematics and Science Education: What Can Be Done Now?* New York: J. C. Crimmins, 1984.

American Association for the Advancement of Science. *Education in the Sciences: A Developing Crisis.* Washington, D.C.: American Association for the Advancement of Science, 1982.

American Association for the Advancement of Science. *What Science Is Most Worth Knowing?* Draft Report of Phase I, Project 2061. Washington, D.C.: American Association for the Advancement of Science, 1987.

American Chemical Society. *Tomorrow: The Report of the Task Force for the Study of Chemistry Education in the United States.* Washington, D.C.: American Chemical Society, 1984.

American Council on Education. *One Third of a Nation.* Report of the Commission on Minority Participation in Education and American Life. Washington, D.C.: American Council on Education, 1988.

Association of American Colleges. *Integrity in the College Curriculum.* Washington, D.C.: Association of American Colleges, 1985.

Baratz, Joan C. *Black Participation in the Teacher Pool.* New York: Carnegie Forum on Education and the Economy, 1986.

Bennett, William J. *James Madison High School: A Curriculum for American Students.* Washington, D.C.: U.S. Department of Education, 1987.

Bennett, William J. *To Reclaim a Legacy.* Washington, D.C.: National Endowment for the Humanities, 1984.

Board on Mathematical Sciences, Panel on Mathematical Sciences, Commission on Physical Sciences, Mathematics, and Resources, National Research Council. *Mathematical Sciences: A Unifying and Dynamic Resource.* Washington, D.C.: National Academy Press, 1986.

Board on Mathematical Sciences, Commission on Physical Sciences, Mathematics, and Resources, National Research Council. *Mathematical Sciences: Some Research Trends.* Washington, D.C.: National Academy Press, 1988.

Board on Mathematical Sciences. "Mathematics: The Unifying Thread in Science." *Notices of the American Mathematical Society,* 33 (1986), 716-733.

Boyer, Ernest L. *High School: A Report on Secondary Education in America.* New York: Harper & Row, 1983.

Boyer, Ernest L. *College: The Undergraduate Experience.* New York: Harper & Row, 1987.

Browder, William (ed.). "Report of the Research Briefing Panel on Mathematics." *Research Briefings 1983.* Research Briefing Panel on Mathematics, Committee on Science, Engineering, and Public Policy, National Academy of Sciences, National Academy of Engineering, Institute of Medicine. Washington, D.C.: National Academy Press, 1983, 1-18.

Burton, Leone. "Mathematical Thinking: The Struggle for Meaning." *Journal for Research in Mathematics Education,* 15:4 (January 1984), 35-49.

Byrd, Jr., Manford. *Implementation Handbook for the Comprehensive Mathematics Program: Kindergarten–Grade 8.* Chicago, Ill.: Board of Education, City of Chicago, 1987.

California Round Table on Educational Opportunity. *Statement on Competencies in English and Mathematics Expected of Entering Freshmen.* Sacramento, Calif.: California State Department of Education, 1982.

Carnegie Forum on Education and the Economy. *A Nation Prepared: Teachers for the 21st Century.* Report of the Task Force on Teaching as a Profession. New York: Carnegie Corporation, 1986.

Carnegie Foundation for the Advancement of Teaching. *Report Card on School Reform.* Carnegie Foundation for the Advancement of Teaching, 1988.

Case, Bettye Anne. *Teaching Assistants and Part-time Instructors.* Washington, D.C.: Mathematical Association of America, 1988.

Chambers, Donald L. *A Guide to Curriculum Planning in Mathematics.* Madison, Wis.: Wisconsin Department of Public Instruction, 1986.

Charles, R. and Silver, E. (eds.). *Teaching and Evaluating Mathematical Problem Solving.* Reston, Va.: National Council of Teachers of Mathematics, 1988.

Cockcroft, Wilfred H. *Mathematics Counts.* London: Her Majesty's Stationery Office, 1986.

College Entrance Examination Board. *Academic Preparation in Mathematics: Teaching for Transition from High School to College.* New York: The College Board, 1985.

Committee on the Undergraduate Program in Mathematics. *Recommendations for a General Mathematical Sciences Program.* Washington, D.C.: Mathematical Association of America, 1981.

Committee on the Undergraduate Program in Mathematics, Panel on Teacher Training. *Recommendations on the Mathematical Preparation of Teachers.* MAA Notes No. 2. Washington, D.C.: Mathematical Association of America, 1983.

Conference Board of the Mathematical Sciences. *New Goals for Mathematical Sciences Education.* Washington, D.C.: Conference Board of the Mathematical Sciences, 1984.

Conference Board of the Mathematical Sciences. "The Mathematical Sciences Curriculum K–12: What Is Still Fundamental and What Is Not." In *Educating Americans for the 21st Century: Source Materials.* National Science Board Commission on Precollege Education in Mathematics, Science, and Technology. Washington, D.C.: National Science Foundation, 1983, 1-23.

Connors, Edward A. "A Decline in Mathematics Threatens Science—and the U.S." *The Scientist,* 2:22 (November 28, 1988), 9, 12.

References

Cooney, Thomas J. "A Beginning Teacher's View of Problem Solving." *Journal for Research in Mathematics Education,* 16 (1985), 324-336.

Cooney, Thomas J. "The Issue of Reform: What Have We Learned from Yesteryear?" *Mathematics Teacher,* 81 (May 1988), 352-363.

Council of Chief State School Officers. *Equity and Excellence: A Dual Thrust in Mathematics and Science Education: Model State Education Agency Efforts.* Washington, D.C.: Council of Chief State School Officers, 1987.

Coyle, Susan L. and Syverson, Peter D. (eds.). *Summary Report 1984: Doctorate Recipients from United States Universities.* Office of Scientific and Engineering Personnel, National Research Council. Washington, D.C.: National Academy Press, 1986.

Crosswhite, F. Joe, et al. *Second International Mathematics Study: Summary Report for the United States.* Washington, D.C.: National Center for Education Statistics, 1985.

Crosswhite, F. Joe, et al. *Second International Mathematics Study: Detailed Report for the United States.* Champaign, Ill.: Stipes Publishing Company, 1986.

D'Ambrosio, Ubiratan. "Uniting Reality and Action: A Holistic Approach to Mathematics Education." In Lynn Arthur Steen and Donald J. Albers (eds.): *Teaching Teachers, Teaching Students: Reflections on Mathematical Education.* Boston, Mass.: Birkhauser Boston, 1981, 33-42.

David, Jr., Edward E. (ed.). *Renewing U.S. Mathematics: Critical Resource for the Future.* Ad Hoc Committee on Resources for the Mathematical Sciences, Commission on Physical Sciences, Mathematics, and Resources, National Research Council. Washington, D.C.: National Academy Press, 1984.

David, Jr., Edward E. "Renewing U.S. Mathematics: An Agenda to Begin the Second Century." *Notices of the American Mathematical Society,* 35 (October 1988), 1119-1123.

Davis, Philip J. "Applied Mathematics as Social Contract." *Mathematics Magazine,* 61:3 (1988), 139-147.

Davis, Robert B. *Learning Mathematics: The Cognitive Science Approach to Mathematics Education.* Norwood, N.J.: Ablex, 1984.

Davis-Van Atta, David, et al. *Educating America's Scientists: The Role of the Research College.* Oberlin, Ohio: Oberlin College, 1985.

Denham, Walter F. and O'Malley, Edward T. (eds.). *Mathematics Framework for California Public Schools, Kindergarten Through Grade Twelve.* Sacramento, Calif.: California State Department of Education, 1985.

Dessart, Donald J. and Suydam, Marilyn N. *Classroom Ideas from Research on Secondary School Mathematics.* Reston, Va.: National Council of Teachers of Mathematics, 1983.

Dossey, John A. "Learning, Teaching, and Standards." *Mathematics Teacher,* 81 (1988), 290-293.

Dossey, John A.; Mullis, Ina V. S.; Lindquist, Mary M.; Chambers, Donald L. *The Mathematics Report Card: Are We Measuring Up?* Princeton, N. J.: Educational Testing Service, 1988.

Driscoll, Mark. *Stories of Excellence: Ten Case Studies from a Study of Exemplary Mathematics Programs.* Reston, Va.: National Council of Teachers of Mathematics, 1987.

Feigenbaum, Mitchell J. and Kruskal, Martin (eds.). "Order, Chaos, and Patterns: Aspects of Nonlinearity." *Research Briefings 1987.* Research Briefing Panel on Order, Chaos, and Patterns: Aspects of Nonlinearity, Committee on Science, Engineering, and Public Policy, National Academy of Sciences, National Academy of Engineering, Institute of Medicine. Washington, D.C.: National Academy Press, 1988.

Fey, James T. *Mathematics Teaching Today: Perspectives from Three National Surveys.* Reston, Va.: National Council of Teachers of Mathematics, 1981.

Fey, James T. (ed.), et al. *Computing and Mathematics: The Impact on Secondary School Curricula.* Reston, Va.: National Council of Teachers of Mathematics, 1984.

Flanders, James. "How Much of the Content in Mathematics Textbooks Is New?" *Arithmetic Teacher,* 35:1 (September 1987), 18-23.

Ford Foundation. *And Gladly Teach: A Ford Foundation Report on Urban Mathematics Collaboratives.* New York: The Ford Foundation, 1987.

Ford Foundation. *Minorities and Mathematics.* New York: A Ford Foundation Staff Paper, 1986.

Freudenthal, Hans. "Major Problems of Mathematics Education." In M. Zweng, et al. (eds.): *Proceedings of the Fourth International Congress on Mathematical Education.* Boston, Mass.: Birkhauser Boston, 1983, 1-7.

Freudenthal, Hans. *Mathematics as an Educational Task.* Norwell, Mass.: Reidel, 1973.

Galambos, Eva C. *Engineering and High Technology Manpower Shortages: The Connection with Mathematics.* Atlanta, Ga.: Southern Regional Education Board, 1980.

General Accounting Office. *New Directions for Federal Programs to Aid Mathematics and Science Teaching.* Washington, D.C.: U.S. Government Printing Office, 1984.

Gilfeather, Frank. "University Support for Mathematical Research." *Notices of the American Mathematical Society,* 34 (November 1987), 1067-1070.

Ginsburg, H. P. (ed.). *The Development of Mathematical Thinking.* New York: Academic Press, 1983.

Gleick, James. *Chaos.* New York: Viking Press, 1987.

Government-University-Industry Research Roundtable, National Academy of Sciences, National Academy of Engineering, Institute of Medicine. *Nurturing Science and Engineering Talent: A Discussion Paper.* Washington, D.C.: National Academy of Sciences, July 1987.

Graham, William R. "Challenges to the Mathematics Community." *Notices of the American Mathematical Society,* 34 (February 1987), 245-250.

Grouws, Douglas A.; Cooney, Thomas J.; Jones, Douglas (eds.). *Perspectives on Research on Effective Mathematics Teaching, Volume 1.* Reston, Va.: National Council of Teachers of Mathematics, 1988.

Harnisch, Delwyn L., et al. "Cross-National Differences in Mathematics Attitude and Achievement Among Seventeen-Year-Olds." *International Journal of Educational Development,* 6:4 (1986), 233-244.

Heckert, Richard E. (chrm.). *High Schools and the Changing Workplace: The Employers' View.* Panel on Secondary School Education for the Changing Workplace, Committee on Science, Engineering and Public Policy, National Academy of Sciences, National Academy of Engineering, Institute of Medicine. Washington, D.C.: National Academy Press, 1984.

References

Heppenheimer, T. A. "Mathematicians at the Receiving End." *Mosaic,* 16:4 (1985), 37-47.

Hirsch, Christian R. and Zweng, Marilyn J. (eds.). *The Secondary School Mathematics Curriculum: 1985 National Council of Teachers of Mathematics Yearbook.* Reston, Va.: National Council of Teachers of Mathematics, 1985.

Hodgkinson, Harold L. *All One System: Demographics of Education—Kindergarten Through Graduate School.* Washington, D.C.: Institute for Educational Leadership, 1985.

Holmes Group. *Tomorrow's Teachers: Report of the Holmes Group.* East Lansing, Mich.: Michigan State University, 1986.

Howson, Geoffrey; Kahane, J.-P.; Lauginie, P.; de Turckheim, E. (eds.). *Mathematics as a Service Subject.* International Commission on Mathematical Instruction Study Series. Cambridge: Cambridge University Press, 1988.

Howson, Geoffrey and Kahane, J.-P. (eds.). *The Influence of Computers and Informatics on Mathematics and Its Teaching.* International Commission on Mathematical Instruction Study Series. Cambridge: Cambridge University Press, 1986.

Howson, Geoffrey and Wilson, Bryan (eds.). *School Mathematics in the 1990s.* International Commission on Mathematical Instruction Study Series. Cambridge: Cambridge University Press, 1986.

"Human Capital: The Decline of America's Work Force." *Business Week,* Special Report, September 19, 1988, 100-141.

International Association for the Evaluation of Educational Achievement. *Science Achievement in Seventeen Countries.* Oxford: Pergamon Press, 1988.

International Commission on Mathematical Instruction. *New Trends in Mathematics Teaching, Volume IV.* Paris: United Nations Educational, Cultural, and Scientific Organization, 1979.

James, H. Thomas and Glaser, Robert. *The Nation's Report Card: Improving the Assessment of Student Achievement.* Cambridge, Mass.: National Academy of Education, 1987.

Johnston, William B. and Packer, Arnold E. (eds.). *Workforce 2000: Work and Workers for the Twenty-First Century.* Indianapolis, Ind.: Hudson Institute, 1987.

Jones, Lyle V.; Lindzey, Gardner; Coggeshall, Porter E. (eds.). *An Assessment of Research Doctorate Programs in the United States: Mathematical and Physical Sciences.* Committee on an Assessment of Quality-Related Characteristics of Research-Doctorate Programs in the United States, National Research Council. Washington, D.C.: National Academy Press, 1982.

Kelly, James A. *Financing Education Reform.* New York: Carnegie Forum on Education and the Economy, 1986.

Kilpatrick, Jeremy. "Inquiry in the Mathematics Classroom." *Academic Connections,* The College Board (1987), 1-2.

Kirsch, Irwin S. and Jungeblut, Ann. *Literacy Profiles of America's Young Adults.* Princeton, N.J.: Educational Testing Service, 1986.

Knapp, Michael S., et al. *Opportunities for Strategic Investment in K-12 Science Education, Volume 1: Problems and Opportunities.* Menlo Park, Calif: SRI International, 1987.

Koerner, James D. (ed.). *The New Liberal Arts: An Exchange of Views.* New York: Alfred P. Sloan Foundation, 1981.

Kozlov, Alex. "Urban Mathematics Collaboratives: Getting Teachers Plugged in." *SIAM News* (September 1987), 24.

Lampert, Magdalene. "Knowing, Doing, and Teaching Mathematics." *Cognition and Instruction,* 3:4 (1986), 305-342.

Lesh, Richard (ed.). *Acquisition of Mathematics Concepts and Processes.* New York: Academic Press, 1983.

Lucas, William F. "New Directions for Undergraduate Mathematics." In Lynn Arthur Steen (ed.): *Mathematics Curriculum Conference.* Northfield, Minn.: St. Olaf College, 1980, 1-21.

Madison, Bernard L. and Hart, Therese A. "Supply, Utilization and Prospects of Talent from the Mathematical Sciences in U.S. Colleges and Universities." (Draft). Committee on the Mathematical Sciences in the Year 2000, Mathematical Sciences Education Board and Board on Mathematical Sciences, Commission on Physical Sciences, Mathematics, and Resources, National Research Council. Washington, D.C.: National Academy Press (forthcoming).

Malcom, Shirley M. *Equity and Excellence: Compatible Goals.* Washington, D.C.: American Association for the Advancement of Science, 1984.

Mason, J.; Burton, L.; Stacey, K. *Thinking Mathematically.* Reading, Mass.: Addison-Wesley, 1982.

Mathematical Association of America. *PRIME-80: Proceedings of the Conference on Prospects in Mathematics Education in the 1980's.* Washington, D.C.: Mathematical Association of America, 1978.

Mathematical Sciences Education Board, National Research Council. *The Teacher of Mathematics: Issues for Today and Tomorrow. Proceedings of a Conference.* Washington, D.C.: National Research Council, 1987.

Maurer, Stephen B. "The Effects of a New College Mathematics Curriculum on High School Mathematics." In Ralston, Anthony and Young, Gail S. (eds.): *The Future of College Mathematics.* New York: Springer-Verlag, 1983, 153-175.

May, Kenneth O. and Schuster, Seymour (eds.). *Undergraduate Research in Mathematics.* Northfield, Minn.: Carleton College, 1961.

McBay, Shirley M. *Increasing the Number and Quality of Minority Science and Mathematics Teachers.* New York: Carnegie Forum on Education and the Economy, 1986.

McKnight, Curtis C., et al. *The Underachieving Curriculum: Assessing U.S. School Mathematics from an International Perspective.* Champaign, Ill.: Stipes Publishing Company, 1987.

Mestre, Jose. "Why Should Mathematics and Science Teachers Be Interested in Cognitive Research Findings?" *Academic Connections,* The College Board (1987), 3-5, 8-11.

Miller, George A. "The Challenge of Universal Literacy." *Science,* 241 (September 9, 1988), 1293-1299.

Mosaic. "Education and the Professional Workforce: A *Mosaic* Special." *Mosaic,* 18:1 (Spring), 1987.

References

Murnane, Richard J. and Raizen, Senta A. (eds.). *Improving Indicators of the Quality of Science and Mathematics Education in Grades K-12.* Committee on Indicators of Precollege Science and Mathematics Education, Commission on Behavioral and Social Sciences and Education, National Research Council. Washington, D.C.: National Academy Press, 1988.

National Advisory Committee on Mathematics Education. *Overview and Analysis of School Mathematics, Grades K-12.* Washington, D.C.: Conference Board of the Mathematical Sciences, 1975.

National Commission on Excellence in Education. *A Nation at Risk: The Imperative for Educational Reform.* Washington, D.C.: U.S. Government Printing Office, 1983.

National Council of Teachers of Mathematics. *An Agenda for Action: Recommendations for School Mathematics of the 1980s.* Reston, Va.: National Council of Teachers of Mathematics, 1980.

National Council of Teachers of Mathematics. *Curriculum and Evaluation Standards for School Mathematics.* Reston, Va.: National Council of Teachers of Mathematics, 1989.

National Council of Teachers of Mathematics. *Priorities in School Mathematics: Executive Summary of the PRISM Project.* Reston, Va.: National Council of Teachers of Mathematics, 1981.

National Council of Teachers of Mathematics. *The Impact of Computing Technology on School Mathematics.* Report of a Conference. Reston, Va.: National Council of Teachers of Mathematics, 1986.

National Governors' Association. *Results in Education 1987: The Governors' 1991 Report on Education.* Washington, D.C.: National Governors' Association, 1987.

National Institute of Education. *Involvement in Learning: Realizing the Potential of American Higher Education.* Washington, D.C.: National Institute of Education, 1984.

National Science Board Commission on Precollege Education in Mathematics, Science and Technology. *Educating Americans for the 21st Century.* Washington, D.C.: National Science Foundation, 1983.

National Science Board Commission on Precollege Education in Mathematics, Science and Technology. *Today's Problems, Tomorrow's Crises.* Washington, D.C.: National Science Foundation, 1982.

National Science Board. *Science and Engineering Education for the 1980s and Beyond.* Washington, D.C.: National Science Foundation, 1980.

National Science Board Task Committee on Undergraduate Science and Engineering Education. *Undergraduate Science, Mathematics and Engineering Education.* Washington, D.C.: National Science Foundation, March 1986.

National Science Board Task Committee on Undergraduate Science and Engineering Education. *Undergraduate Science, Mathematics and Engineering Education, Volume II: Source Materials.* Washington, D.C.: National Science Foundation, November 1987.

National Science Foundation. *What Are the Needs in Precollege Science, Mathematics, and Social Science Education? Views from the Field.* Washington, D.C.: National Science Foundation, 1979.

National Science Foundation. *Women and Minorities in Science and Engineering.* Washington, D.C.: National Science Foundation, 1988.

Naumer, Jr., Walter W.; Sanders, Ted. *State Goals for Learning and Sample Learning Objectives: Mathematics, Grades 3, 6, 8, 10, 12.* Springfield, Ill.: Illinois State Board of Education, 1986.

Nisbett, Richard E., et al. "Teaching Reasoning." *Science,* 238 (October 30, 1987), 625-631.

Norman, Colin. "Math Education: A Mixed Picture." *Science,* 241 (July 22, 1988), 408-409.

Oaxaca, Jaime and Reynolds, Ann W. *Changing America: The New Face of Science and Engineering.* (Interim Report.) Washington, D.C.: Task Force on Women, Minorities, and the Handicapped in Science and Technology, September 1988.

Office of Technology Assessment. *Educating Scientists and Engineers, Grade School to Grad School.* Washington, D.C.: Office of Technology Assessment, 1988.

Peterson, Ivars. *The Mathematical Tourist: Snapshots of Modern Mathematics.* New York: W. H. Freeman, 1988.

Price, Jack and Gawronski, J. D. (eds.). *Changing School Mathematics: A Responsive Process.* Reston, Va.: National Council of Teachers of Mathematics, 1981.

Ralston, Anthony et al. *A Framework for Revision of the K–12 Mathematics Curriculum.* Task Force Report submitted to the Mathematical Sciences Education Board, National Research Council. Washington, D.C.: National Research Council, 1988.

Ralston, Anthony and Young, Gail S. *The Future of College Mathematics.* New York: Springer-Verlag, 1983.

Resnick, Lauren B. *Education and Learning to Think.* Committee on Mathematics, Science, and Technology Education, Commission on Behavioral and Social Sciences and Education, National Research Council. Washington, D.C.: National Academy Press, 1987.

Resnick, Lauren B. "Mathematics and Science Learning: A New Conception." *Science,* 220 (April 29, 1983), 477-478.

Rheinboldt, Werner C. (ed.). *Computational Modeling and Mathematics Applied to the Physical Sciences.* Committee on the Applications of Mathematics, Office of Mathematical Sciences, Commission on Physical Sciences, Mathematics, and Resources, National Research Council. Washington, D.C.: National Academy Press, 1984.

Rheinboldt, Werner C. *Future Directions in Computational Mathematics, Algorithms, and Scientific Software.* Philadelphia, Pa.: Society for Industrial and Applied Mathematics, 1985.

Romberg, Thomas A. "A Common Curriculum for Mathematics." *Individual Differences and the Common Curriculum: Eighty-Second Yearbook of the National Society for the Study of Education.* Chicago, Ill.: University of Chicago Press, 1983, 124.

Romberg, Thomas A. "Policy Implications of the Three R's of Mathematics Education: Revolution, Reform, and Research." Paper presented at annual meeting of American Educational Research Association, 1988.

Romberg, Thomas A. *School Mathematics: Options for the 1990s.* Chairman's Report of a Conference, Madison, Wisconsin. Washington, D.C.: U. S. Department of Education, 1984.

Romberg, Thomas A. and Stewart, Deborah M. (eds.). *The Monitoring of School Mathematics: Background Papers, V. 1-3.* Madison, Wis.: Wisconsin Center for Education Research, University of Wisconsin, 1987.

References

Sanders, Ted. *Mathematics in Illinois: State of the State, 1984-1985.* Springfield, Ill.: Illinois State Board of Education, 1987.

Schoenfeld, Alan H. (ed.). *Cognitive Science and Mathematics Education.* Hillsdale, N. J.: Erlbaum, 1987.

Schoenfeld, Alan H. *Mathematical Problem Solving.* New York: Academic Press, 1985.

Shulman, Lee S. and Sykes, Gary. *A National Board for Teaching? In Search of a Bold Standard.* New York: Carnegie Forum on Education and the Economy, 1986.

Simon, Barry (ed.). *Report of the Committee on American Graduate Mathematics Enrollments.* Washington, D.C.: Conference Board of the Mathematical Sciences, 1987.

Smith, David A.; Porter, Gerald J.; Leinbach, L. Carl; Wenger, Ronald H. (eds.). *Computers and Mathematics: The Use of Computers in Undergraduate Instruction.* MAA Notes No. 9. Washington, D.C.: Mathematical Association of America, 1988.

State Education Assessment Center. *Recommendations on Developing Science/Mathematics Indicators with the States and Year-One Report of the Project.* Washington, D.C.: Council of Chief State School Officers, 1987.

State Education Assessment Center. *State Education Policies Related to Science and Mathematics.* Washington, D.C.: Council of Chief State School Officers, 1987.

State University of New York. *Three-Year Sequence for High School Mathematics, Course I-III.* New York: University of the State of New York, The State Education Department, 1983.

Steen, Lynn Arthur. "A Time of Transition: Mathematics for the Middle Grades." In R. Lodholz (ed.): *A Change in Emphasis.* Parkway, Mo.: Parkway School District, 1986, 1-9.

Steen, Lynn Arthur (ed.). *Calculus for a New Century: A Pump, Not a Filter.* MAA Notes No. 8. Washington, D.C.: Mathematical Association of America, 1988.

Steen, Lynn Arthur. "Mathematics Education: A Predictor of Scientific Competitiveness." *Science,* 237 (July 17, 1987), 251-252, 302.

Steen, Lynn Arthur. "The Science of Patterns." *Science,* 240 (April 29, 1988), 611-616.

Steen, Lynn Arthur and Albers, Donald J. (eds.). *Teaching Teachers, Teaching Students: Reflections on Mathematical Education.* Boston, Mass.: Birkhauser Boston, 1981.

Stevenson, Harold W., et al. "Mathematics Achievement of Chinese, Japanese, and American Children." *Science,* 231 (February 14, 1986), 693-699.

Stewart, William L. (dir.). *Foreign Citizens in U.S. Science and Engineering: History, Status, and Outlook.* Washington, D.C.: National Science Foundation, 1987.

Tammadge, Alan and Starr, Phyllis. *A Parents' Guide to School Mathematics.* School Mathematics Project Handbooks. Cambridge: Cambridge University Press, 1977.

Taylor, John L. (ed.). *Teacher Shortage in Science and Mathematics: Myths, Realities, and Research.* Washington, D.C.: National Institute of Education, 1984.

Thompson, A. G. "The Relationship of Teachers' Conceptions of Mathematics and Mathematics Teaching to Instructional Practice." *Educational Studies in Mathematics,* 15 (1984), 105-127.

Tobias, Sheila. "Insiders and Outsiders." *Academic Connections.* The College Board (Winter 1988), 1-5.

Turner, Nura and Rains, Dorothea. *Careers of Mathematically Talented Students: A 27-Year Study of Top-Rankers in the 1958-1960 AHSME,* 1986.

Tyson-Bernstein, Harriet. *A Conspiracy of Good Intentions: America's Textbook Fiasco.* Washington, D.C.: Council for Basic Education, 1988.

Weiss, Iris R. "Middle School Mathematics Teachers: Results from the 1985-86 National Survey of Science and Mathematics Education." Office of Opportunities in Science, American Association for the Advancement of Science, November 1987.

What Works: Research About Teaching and Learning. Washington, D.C.: U. S. Department of Education, 1986.

What Works: Schools That Work, Educating Disadvantaged Children. Washington, D.C.: U.S. Department of Education, 1987.

Widnall, Sheila E. "AAAS Presidential Lecture: Voices from the Pipeline." *Science,* 241 (September 30, 1988), 1740-1745.

Wilf, Herbert S. "The Disk with the College Education." *American Mathematical Monthly,* 89 (1982), 4-8.

Willoughby, Stephen S. *Teaching Mathematics: What Is Basic?* Occasional Paper 31. Washington, D.C.: Council for Basic Education, 1981.

Wirszup, Izaak and Streit, Robert (eds.). *Developments in School Mathematics Education Around the World.* Reston, Va.: National Council of Teachers of Mathematics, 1987.

Zorn, Paul. "Computing in Undergraduate Mathematics." *Notices of the American Mathematical Society,* 34 (October 1987), 917-923.

Credits for *EVERYBODY COUNTS*

Composition contributed by the American Mathematical Society.

Editorial coordination by Audrey Pendergast.

Graphic design by Permut & Associates.

Services of models on cover contributed by Camera-Ready Kids Talent Management.

Cover photography by Bochicchio Photography.

Illustration by Mark Stutzman, Eloqui.

Photographs courtesy of: p. xiv-NASA; p. 1-NASA; p. 15-Wisconsin Center for Education Research; p. 16-Danny Lyon, EPA-Documerica; p. 17-U.S. Congress, Office of Technology Assessment, *Educating Scientists and Engineers: Grade School to Grad School,* OTA-SET-377, Washington, D.C.: U.S. Government Printing Office, June 1988, p. 95; p. 20-Tom Keller/The Foundation for Advancements in Science and Education; p. 24-Godfrey Argent; p. 30-Charles Frizzell/Wisconsin Center for Education Research; p. 31-The George Washington University; p. 42-Carl Zitzmann/George Mason University; p. 43-Houston Independent School District (blind teacher and blind student); p. 55-The George Washington University; p. 56-Wisconsin Center for Education Research; p. 57 - The George Washington University; p. 71-Wisconsin Center for Education Research; p. 72-The George Washington University; p. 73-Wisconsin Center for Education Research; p. 85-H.-O. Peitgen and P. H. Richter, *The Beauty of Fractals,* Berlin: Springer-Verlag, 1986, p. 22; p. 86-Katherine Lambert/Special Projects Division, National Science Teachers Association (Erich Bloch, Director, National Science Foundation and Sue Poole White, Washington, D.C., mathematics teacher, winner of 1987 Presidential Award for Excellence in Science and Mathematics Teaching); p. 87-Special Projects Division, National Science Teachers Association; p. 98-Houston Independent School District; p. 99-The George Washington University.